INSOLVENCY IN BUSINESS: how to avoid it, how to deal with it

INSOLVENCY IN BUSINESS:
how to avoid it, how to deal with it

PAUL FINN

CASSELL

Cassell Educational Limited
Villiers House,
41/47 Strand,
London, WC2N 5JE

First published 1989
Reprinted with additions 1990

British Library Cataloguing in Publication Data
Finn, Paul
INSOLVENCY IN BUSINESS: how to avoid it, how to
deal with it.
1. England. Insolvency. Law
I. Title
344.206'78
ISBN 0-304-31797-7

Typeset in Bodoni by Chapterhouse of Formby, Lancs.
Printed and bound by
Biddles Ltd., Guildford and King's Lynn.

To the memory of David Charles Horton
('dear old Horty'), a good friend and most able
insolvency practitioner, sadly missed, who,
as a former partner, and for all the
wrong reasons at the time, set me along the
path of the insolvency practitioner. Without him
this book could not have been written.

CONTENTS

Preface   ix

1 Limited Liability?   1
The Concept of Limited Liability   2
The Road to Corporate Insolvency   2
Preventative Measures   2
The Crossroads   6
Directorship – the Pitfalls   6
The Answer – Emergency Plan B (EPB)   10
Summary   12

2 Corporate Insolvency   13
Which Way Forward?   14
Receivership   15
Administration Order   43
Liquidation   49
Summary   53

3 Bankruptcy – The Avoidable Option   54
Background   55
The Road to Bankruptcy   55
The Option BC   56
The Options AD   57
Deeds of Arrangement   58
The Voluntary Arrangement   61
Preferences and Transfers at Undervalue   62
Summary   63

4 Common Considerations   66
Personal Guarantees   67
Meetings of Creditors   72
Statements of Affairs   78
Vanishing Deposits   92
The Poor Man Investor   94

5 Stories from the Author's Diary   97
Fred's Downfall   98
The Over-secured Joint and Several Guarantee   99
The Petition that Backfired   102
Directors' Unlimited Liability   105
Bankruptcy – the Avoidable Option?   105

6 Insolvency in Business – How to Avoid it   108
Starting a New Business   108
How to Avoid Financial Failure   114

Epilogue   119
Index   120

The illustration on page 65 is reproduced by permission of the British Library.

PREFACE

It was in the mid 1980s that I first became aware of a need to advise potential bankrupts that there was at least a chance of avoiding formal bankruptcy. This followed my own discovery that in one particular year my manager and I had, between us, taken almost one quarter of all the country's appointments as Trustee in Deeds of Arrangement. Given the small number of appointments involved, it seemed evident that there had to be many a Poor Man (sole trader or small businessman) who might have been saved from bankruptcy had someone only troubled to tell him there was a possible alternative.

Since then we have had the new insolvency legislation in 1985 and 1986 and with it, perhaps, a greater general awareness. What we have also, however, are new pitfalls facing company directors which could, under certain circumstances, place them on the road to personal bankruptcy. It therefore seemed logical to look at insolvency on a broader basis and to try to deal not just with personal bankruptcy but also with the position of companies and their directors. It is hoped that through a greater awareness of some of the problems and the pitfalls which face any businessman, his arrival at the road to bankruptcy might be avoided and the book's orignal *raison d'être* rendered unnecessary.

To achieve this I have had to expand considerably upon my original concept, which now appears as chapter 3 of the book, representing, I think, the logical order of progression down the road to insolvency.

In order to keep the technical detail to a minimum, it has been necessary to restrict the text to cover the current law in England. Scotland has its own variations; for example, there is no equivalent office in Scotland of England's Official Receiver: nor do Scottish banks take fixed charges over book debts. Thus, although the basic principles of insolvency are the same in Scotland as they are in England, care should be taken north of the border to consult with a solicitor or licensed insolvency practitioner conversant with current Scottish law. (The Insolvency Act 1986 refers to insolvency practitioners as being 'authorised' to act, but the practitioners will more usually refer to themselves as 'licensed'.)

Insolvency is a serious, not a humorous topic. There is nothing funny about money problems; I have been close witness to the financial difficulties of too many individuals to be under any illusion on that score. I nevertheless believe that any subject, however serious, does not have to be approached in a doom-laden or over-grave manner. Indeed, it is remarkable how many Poor Men whilst having lost their money have yet managed to retain their sense of humour. After all, with a little luck they are going to sort out their problems and have a fresh start without the continuing burden of debt.

I saw my main task as to make what is necessarily a complicated subject as basically understandable and readable as possible, thereby encouraging the reader to finish the book. An unread textbook, however serious, is of little use to anyone. That said, I hope that no financially troubled reader will be offended by my deliberately chosen style.

The drawings are intended to complement the message and for these I am indebted to Peter Bentley and YPL Public Relations of Tong Hall, Bradford.

My thanks also to my own insolvency staff for their constructive criticism and especially to Ian Fletcher W.S. of Richards Butler, Solicitors, London, for reading the text.

The responsibility for any mistake which might occur in the text remains, however, entirely mine.

PHF *November 1988*

1 Limited Liability?

The Concept of Limited Liability

The concept of limited liability goes back over a hundred years and was introduced to afford a measure of protection to sole traders when business failures – and ensuing bankruptcies – were rife.

The intention was to remove at least some of the risk of capital loss from the individual and spread it amongst his creditors – who could balance their anticipated profits arising from trading with the company against the likelihood of loss in the event of the company's failing.

As we proceed along the road to corporate insolvency, we will discover that whereas it has always been possible under certain circumstances for a creditor to penetrate the shield of limited liability (though usually with the greatest of difficulty), legislation, commencing with the Insolvency Act 1985, opened up new areas which leave the Poor Man (company) director (PMD) far more exposed. In other words, the law now places further limitations upon the original concept of limited liability.

The Road to Corporate Insolvency

In the ensuing text we are concerned with the Poor Man who, whether through bad luck, bad judgment or some blend of this, finds himself requiring specialist help. Those who prey on the innocent whilst utilising the shelter of limited liability to protect themselves require a different kind of assistance.

It is a fact that many successful businesses have been built up following earlier failures, the Poor Man having taken on board lessons learned and avoided the pitfalls the second time.

It might, therefore, be helpful to start at the beginning so that even if our Poor Man in question is already way down the road to insolvency, he might be in a position to give further heed to the areas of prevention in any renaissance.

At this stage, however, we will restrict our 'Preventative Measures' to those simple but vital areas which every trading business ought to address. For the Poor Man Entrepreneur (PME) who is contemplating starting up in business or is looking to develop a degree of commercial awareness, chapter 6 covers these wider aspects in further detail.

Preventative Measures

'Prevention is better than cure.' How many times have we heard that expression – and how aptly it applies to the road to insolvency.

Surely the first step that any prudent company director must take is

2

to minimise the possibility of bad debts – which, in turn, might have the effect of making his own company insolvent?

Few companies can afford to employ the full-time services of an experienced credit controller, but this does not mean that this vital aspect of control should not be given top priority *before* granting credit to customers and potential customers.

Until 1967 the Poor Man was denied access to any accounting information concerning the majority of his customers, who would have been exempt from filing their accounts at Companies House.

The Companies Act 1967 altered all that, but for subsequent years the average company delayed filing its accounts until long after the legal period of grace allowed. This has been particularly true of those companies who were potentially a credit risk.

The Registrar of Companies, with computer help, has made noticeable strides towards tightening up on those who delay in filing information required by statute. Even so, given that every company is allowed ten months following its year-end in which to file the required information, it is possible that the Poor Man searching the current register could be looking at information which covers an accounting period ended twenty-one months previously.

The only sane, safe way forward is for the Poor Man to enlist skilled help to supplement his own efforts; thus:

1 He should by all means ask the prospective customer to supply two trade references, *but also*:

2 Consider asking his solicitor or accountant to recommend a reputable trade protection association to make enquiries on his behalf and issue a credit status report upon his prospective customers.

It is, of course, possible that such an association might not

3

have up-to-the-minute information (his own prospective customer may have suffered a crippling bad debt the previous
day, with no chance for that information to have filtered
through) but it will be in a far stronger position than the Poor
Man to evaluate the potential risk.

If, for whatever reason, the Poor Man chooses not to use a
trade protection association, a compromise would be a
request to his accountant or solicitor to arrange a search of his
prospective customer's records at Companies House. This
should at least provide basic information. For example, if the
accounts disclose a weak financial position and particularly if
the company is overdue in filing its accounts, he will know to
proceed with extreme caution. In addition, the Register of
Charges will show to what extent the company's assets have
already been pledged against prior borrowings – for example,
to secure bank loans or overdrafts.

3 If the Poor Man is a supplier of goods – as opposed to services
– he should if possible incorporate into the company's terms
of trade a *reservation of title* clause, so drafted as to keep title
in the goods from passing to the customer until paid for in full
(often referred to as a 'Romalpa' clause after the famous case
Aluminium Industrie Vaasen BV v. *Romalpa Aluminium
Ltd*, which highlighted the principle of being able to retain
title in goods supplied but not paid for).

Once again, this is a highly specialised area where the Poor
Man *must* seek legal advice to ensure that:

a   it is possible to retain title in the goods, given the type of product supplied;

b   the relevant clauses are drafted as widely as possible; even if the goods have been resold it might be possible for the Poor Man's claim to attach to the debt thereby created, if the sub-purchaser of the goods has, in turn, not paid the Poor Man's customer;

c   the clauses are binding upon the customer. For example, they must be seen to have been brought to his attention *before* delivery. It is no good in the case of a single supply for the Poor Man to print his conditions of trade upon the invoice; under normal circumstances they would at the very least need to be incorporated into his acknowledgment of order as a condition of sale.

Having had the necessary clauses drawn up, the safest way to protect against any future argument as to their enforcement is to have the customer sign a document accepting the conditions of trade. What the Poor Man is really saying to his customer is

Mine till you pay – O.K.?

If, having taken all precautions, the Poor Man finds himself in the position of being unable to obtain payment for goods or services supplied, what does he do next?

He should never forget the time-proven adage:

Twice blest he whose cause is just,
Thrice blest he who gets his blow in – fust!

The Poor Man should make no delay in seeking professional advice with a view to enforcing his legal remedies.

His trade protection association, solicitor or, in the initial stage, his accountant, should be able to point him in the right direction – and he might be surprised to learn that there could be more avenues open to him than the good old writ or summons.

One word of warning: it could be dangerous for the Poor Man simply to sit back and hope to be paid – not because he may be disappointed (although he probably *will* be disappointed), but because if the debtor decides to prefer the Poor Man, i.e. pay him in preference to other creditors, he could be called upon to repay the money if his debtor goes into liquidation within six months and it is subsequently established was insolvent at the time of the preference. (The time-scale is extended to two years if the debtor and the Poor Man are associated or if the preference involves a transaction at undervalue.)

Remember, however, that the intention to prefer is in the mind of the payer not the receiver. If the Poor Man insists on payment this *may* be sufficient to remove the chance of a 'preference claim'.

The Crossroads

We have now arrived at that point where many a Poor Man will be joining us; for whatever reason, bad debt, bad judgment or just plain bad luck has brought him to the point where he either 'plays the ostrich', closing his eyes to the company's problems and hoping for the best, or opts for what we will call *Emergency Plan B*, by which we mean that he follows a course which is designed to protect him from criticism or, worse still, an accusation of fraudulent trading or wrongful trading.

Directorship – the Pitfalls

Acting as a director is an onerous responsibility. Ignorance of the law is no excuse; the PMD is presumed and expected to know all that is necessary to discharge his legal responsibilities.

Should the Poor Man attempt to enjoy the authority and the benefits of directorship without the title, he could have a nasty shock if anything goes wrong.

6

The law has anticipated his initiative and he can be caught by the penalties for transgression just as if he openly admitted to being a director.

One title given to a person who acts as a director, by whatever title, is 'shadow' director, but however called, if the Poor Man *acts* as a director then he will be treated in any insolvent liquidation as if he *had* been a director.

There are many duties which a director needs to discharge with due diligence if he is to avoid some sort of problem in an ensuing liquidation of the company. Simple examples would be the need to maintain proper books of account, to file annual returns and accounts promptly with the Registrar of Companies and to remain at all times at arm's length in any transactions with the company in which he may have an interest.

There are others (we will come to some of them shortly), and they are all important. For the moment, however, we are concentrating upon the major pitfalls that could place the PMD upon the road to bankruptcy. There are four such potential pitfalls, namely:

- Acting as a director when disqualified from so acting by the court
- Fraudulent trading
- Wrongful trading
- Personal guarantee

Acting as a director when disqualified

Steps were first taken in 1976 to tighten up earlier legislation whereby a director could be disqualified from acting as a company director on the grounds that his previous conduct rendered him unfit for such office.

Since then the powers of the court have been greatly extended, first of all by virtue of the relevant sections of the Companies Act 1985 and then through legislation contained in the Insolvency Act 1985.

All of this legislation was consolidated into a new Act, the Company Directors Disqualification Act 1986 – which should give the PMD some idea as to the seriousness with which the courts now view directors' responsibilities.

Mention has already been made of certain duties which the PMD must discharge with due diligence.

Some of the more serious offences would include:

- Acting as a director when already disqualified.
- Acting as a director when an undischarged bankrupt.
- Any conviction for an indictable offence in connection with the promotion, formation, management or liquidation of the company.
- Any misfeasance or breach of any fiduciary or other duty. (Wrongful exercise of lawful authority or breach of trust.)
- Any misappropriation or retention of the company's property.
- Any conviction for fraudulent or wrongful trading (see below).

A person who acts as a director when disqualified is personally liable for all the relevant debts of the company.

Fraudulent trading

The PMD was, at least in theory, always at risk if his company became insolvent and a liquidator challenged him through the courts for incurring credit with intent to defraud creditors.

In practice, any claim was difficult to sustain as, by and large, and particularly following a famous judgment on the subject, all the Poor Man had to demonstrate to avoid liability was that he believed 'there was light at the end of the tunnel'.

Cases have, however, been proved against the Poor Man under this heading which have led to awards against him, ordering him to make contribution to the company's creditors from his personal assets. *Thus we have a potential start towards the road to bankruptcy.*

8

The first reported case of an action for wrongful trading brought by a liquidator was *re: Produce Marketing Consortium Limited* (Chancery Division March 1989). This is an important case which established that:

a any award is meant to be compensatory rather than penal; and

b a director could be liable if he was in ignorance, 'not only [of the] facts which a director ought to know but also those which he ought to ascertain'.

It is important to remember that the concept of fraudulent trading has not been replaced; it has been reinforced with additional legislation.

Wrongful trading

The new legislation introduces the concept of *wrongful trading*. In simple terms the PMD could find himself claimed against if he allowed the company to trade when it was insolvent or when he knew or should have concluded that there was no reasonable prospect of the company's avoiding an insolvent liquidation.

It is no answer to a charge of wrongful trading that the PMD plausibly believed 'there was a light at the end of the tunnel'. This would probably have cleared him from the earlier charge of fraudulent trading, but now he needs a different answer.

The answer, which we will consider in a moment, is to follow Emergency Plan B, but before we look at the answer, let us first consider the consequences.

It is inevitable that any PMD found guilty of wrongful trading could face disqualification (for a period of up to the present maximum of fifteen years) from acting as a director. *Secondly, and perhaps of more immediate concern, he faces an order to make payment to the liquidator out of his personal assets, so as to make funds available for creditors generally.*

In coming to a decision, the court will look at the particular background of the individual PMD. It is, for example, likely to come down harder on an insolvent company's financial director, who is a trained accountant, than upon, say, the transport director in the same company who is trained as a long-distance lorry driver. Conversely, however, it will not be sufficient excuse for the Poor Man sole director to disclaim liability on the grounds that he had no formal accountancy training.

Personal guarantee

A guarantor has been described as 'an idiot at the end of a fountain pen'. Like many sayings there may be a degree of truth in it, but any lender would counter by asking why he should be prepared to risk his investors' money if the entrepreneur who stood to gain the profits was not prepared to join in the risk.

There can be specific problems concerning guarantees which are given and supported by charges on personal property, for example the family home.

We will be looking in greater detail at some of the problems associated with guarantees, with particular reference to potential pitfalls where the PMD's personal property is pledged in support of his guarantee, when we come to chapter 4.

Another area of potential pitfall concerns joint and several guarantees (see chapter 4), supported by charged assets. A cautionary tale is related in chapter 5.

However sound the reasons for giving the guarantee, it matters not if the Poor Man director-guarantor is called upon to make payment under its terms and is without sufficient funds – he faces the road to bankruptcy.

The Answer – Emergency Plan B (EPB)

EPB was always the only full answer to any complaint that a director had continued to trade and incur credit when his company was insolvent. Now, short of the appropriate cash injection, or ceasing to trade, it is the *only* answer to a charge of wrongful trading, which requires a director to show that once he knew or should have known or ought to have ascertained that there was no prospect of the company's avoiding insolvent liquidation *he took every step with a view to minimising the potential loss to creditors.*

(Although it may be possible for the PMD to take out special insurance giving protection in the event of a claim by a liquidator, this can be no substitute for good management.)

Stated simply, EPB is the route whereby at the first hint of financial trouble the PMD immediately consults with his solicitor or a licensed insolvency practitioner to seek and act upon their advice as to his next course of action. His adviser should most certainly counsel the preparation of an immediate up-to-date *Statement of Affairs* by independent insolvency accountants. It will be in the light of that statement of affairs that the appropriate advice can then be given.

The first hint of financial trouble

The most common early warning signal is the drying-up of the cash flow, with the inevitable creditor pressure that follows. Until 1985 the *only* definition of insolvency was 'the inability to pay one's debts as and when they fell due'. This situation has now been extended so that a Poor Man or his company may be insolvent where their liabilities (including contingent and prospective liabilities) exceed their assets.

(It is to be hoped that the law will be clarified to establish beyond doubt that contingent liabilities need only be included in the calculations where they are expected to become actual liabilities. Under the present definition, companies with large contingent claims – which would be excluded on a conventional accounting basis – could be regarded as insolvent.)

However trouble manifests itself, the Poor Man should always counter any attempt at an explanation which might point towards a 'light at the end of the tunnel' by applying the acid test and seeking an honest answer to the question, *If things are so good, why are things so bad?* Better still, he should ask his professional advisers to answer the question for him.

However glibly hopeful an initial response may be to trading problems, it is virtually impossible to cheat when this test is applied.

Summary

The protection of limited liability afforded to company directors, whilst never watertight, has since the Insolvency Acts of 1985 and 1986 been significantly eroded.

The only safe way for the PMD to protect himself from sliding down the road to corporate insolvency – which might become the road to personal bankruptcy – is, following the first signs of being in financial difficulties, to:

- Cease to trade immediately, or
- Inject further required capital, or
- Consult a solicitor or licensed insolvency practitioner and follow their advice.

How many times in the past have insolvency practitioners been heard to say, 'If only you'd come to see me sooner, we might have been able to save the business.'? One of the benefits of the PMD's seeking early professional help is that it affords the opportunity for remedial action at a much earlier stage and, therefore, a better chance of preventing an insolvent liquidation.

If some sort of formal insolvency is inevitable, then the company will already be in the hands of an appropriate expert who will be able to take the initiative in protecting the interests of all concerned.

In chapter 2, we will consider the various options available to the creditors of an insolvent company and the alternative formal routes down which the insolvent company may proceed. *If, however, having reached this point, the Poor Man as a company director finds himself on the road to bankruptcy for whatever reason, then he needs now to proceed to chapter 3 of this book.*

2 Corporate Insolvency

Which Way Forward?

There is only one occasion where the directors of an insolvent company have the opportunity to dictate the road forward without reference, at some stage, to the company's creditors. This is when, despite being unable to pay all its debts as and when due, the company will be in a position to satisfy all creditors within a period of twelve months.

Under these circumstances, the directors may swear a Statutory Declaration of Solvency and then place the company into Members' Voluntary Liquidation, appointing their own liquidator (who must be a licensed insolvency practitioner).

One word of warning: the penalties for recklessly swearing a statutory declaration of solvency are very severe; understandably so, because the effect of placing a company into members' voluntary liquidation is to deny the creditors any opportunity of dealing with their claims or taking further action against the company for the period of one year. If there is the slightest doubt as to the ability of the company to meet its liabilities in full and within twelve months, then this route should not be contemplated.

In all other instances, it will be the creditors who ultimately decide the chosen route, although it is usual for the PMD, through his advisers, to attempt to influence his preference of direction – but what are the alternatives?

There are three main routes forward plus two additional branch roads, namely:

Main routes
    1 Receivership
    2 Administration Order
    Branch roads
      a Scheme under Section 425, Companies Act 1985
      b Voluntary Arrangement under Part I, Insolvency Act 1986
    3 Liquidation – which may be
      a Creditors' Voluntary or
      b Compulsory

This section of the book deals, in turn, with each of these options.

Certain aspects of insolvency will arise irrespective of the chosen route. Examples would be the preparation of a Statement of Affairs, the rights of employees, the difference between fixed and floating charges and the significance of being a secured or preferential (as opposed to unsecured) creditor. As our first main route is receivership, it is here that we will first meet those terms.

What we will try not to do, however, is to dwell on them any longer than necessary at this initial stage. To keep the text simple we will identify these individual aspects of insolvency and then enlarge upon them, as Common Considerations, in chapter 4 of the book.

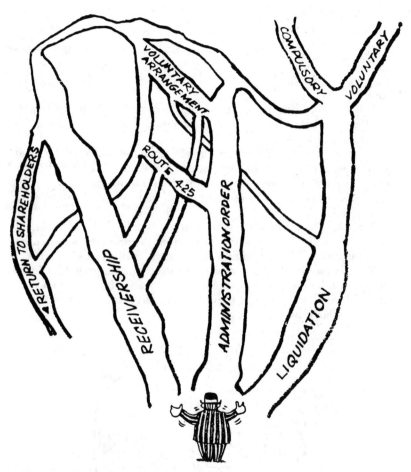

Receivership

Fixed charges
Anyone lending money to a company (as opposed to extending credit)

can require that security be given to safeguard his advance. *It is when he needs to realise that security to recover his debt that we come across the expression 'receivership'. Without security given by way of a charge there can be no receivership.*

The most common forms of security are:

1 Charges over the company's assets; and
2 Security outside the company, normally referred to as 'collateral' or 'third party' security.

Inevitably, it is the banks who are the main suppliers of working capital and, consequently, the main 'takers' of security and they display an understandable preference to see that their monies are well covered!

It is therefore quite common for them to require security under both headings, namely a charge over the company's assets, supported by directors' guarantees.

We have already touched very briefly upon the subject of personal guarantees in chapter 1, but anyone contemplating the giving of a personal guarantee to support a company's borrowing should read chapter 4, where the subject and some of its less obvious pitfalls are considered in more detail.

Most people are familiar with charges over freehold or leasehold properties, which – irrespective of whether the property is owned by the company or the individual PMD – are known as *fixed charges*.

Most house owners have at some time or another granted a fixed charge to a building society or bank in exchange for an advance to enable them either to buy or improve a property and will know them, more familiarly, as a mortgage.

Imagine the position where our PMD has mortgaged his home to raise money, not, in this instance, to assist in its purchase or improvement, but to secure an advance to his business. Now it is one thing for any Poor Man to have to give up his home because he is no longer able to meet his mortgage commitments, but quite another to ask him to move out so that the bank can take possession to pay off a collateral guarantee.

To overcome this problem, the bank has, on occasion, to resort to the legal remedy, available to it under its fixed charge, of appointing a receiver.

Fixed-charge receiver
It is the duty of a receiver appointed under a fixed charge to take possession of the property and sell it at the best possible price in order to pay all monies due to the fixed-charge holder. Only after the costs and fees of the receiver have been met (if the mortgage deed does not otherwise cover the point, the Law of Property Act 1925 allows for fees of up to 5 per cent of the price realised), and all amounts outstanding and due to the fixed-charge holder paid in full, will any balance of the sale proceeds be paid over to the Poor Man guarantor.

A receiver under a fixed charge does not have to be an authorised insolvency practitioner – the one exception to the rule. Logically it often makes sense to appoint an expert in property; often, for example, a chartered surveyor, whose task is to realise the best price for the charged property.

The right of the fixed-charge holder to appoint a receiver subsists irrespective of whether the property is owned by the individual or by the company, but it is unusual (although not unknown) for a fixed-charge receiver to be appointed to a company. Banks, in particular, will usually prefer to appoint a different kind of receiver known as an 'administrative receiver', the reasons for which we will now consider.

It is possible for a lender to take fixed charges over assets other than freehold or leasehold property and, where a bank lends money to a company, it is usual for it to take fixed charges over:

- the company's freehold and leasehold properties
- any fixed plant and machinery (as opposed to moveable plant – a legal distinction often difficult to establish)
- book debts (that is, monies due to the company from whatever source, but will usually be mainly for goods or services supplied and not yet paid for)
- goodwill, and
- uncalled share capital

This last asset, not often come across in practice, arises when shareholders have subscribed for (agreed to buy) shares issued by the company but have either not paid for them or have paid only one or more part instalments, referred to as 'calls'. The outstanding balance is an asset over which it is possible to take a fixed charge.

Floating charges and administrative receivers

A bank will always look to its fixed charges as its main source of security. This is because it has an absolute right to the proceeds of any realisation. As we will learn when we read about guarantees in chapter 4, even the Inland Revenue cannot intervene to collect any capital gains tax which might arise from a sale of an asset covered by a fixed charge.

Also important, however, are *floating charges*, which in effect 'float' or 'hover' over assets which, by their very nature, are either constantly changing or are of a less permanent nature than fixed-charge assets. Such charges crystallise upon the actual assets held by the company at the moment the charge holder calls in his security.

Assets generally covered by a floating charge will include:

- stocks
- work in progress
- fixtures and fittings
- motor vehicles not on lease or hire-purchase, and
- non-fixed plant and machinery.

Floating-charge assets are of secondary importance to a bank as security to cover advances, because they must be applied firstly in paying the company's preferential creditors. Only once these preferential creditors have been satisfied in full is any surplus then available towards the bank borrowings.

The main preferential creditors are, in general terms:

- Customs and Excise for up to six months' arrears of Value Added Tax (VAT)
- Inland Revenue for up to twelve months' arrears of Pay As You Earn (PAYE)
- Department of Health and Social Security for up to twelve months' arrears of National Insurance Contributions (NIC)
- Employees for arrears of holiday pay and (with a current maximum of £800 per employee) up to four months' arrears of wages.

We will come across preferential creditors again when we consider the Statement of Affairs in chapter 4.

These fixed and floating charges which, to be effective, have to be registered at Companies House, are embodied in a document called a *debenture*, which will normally contain provisions for the lender – or debenture holder – to appoint an administrative receiver (AR). *Now we have arrived at our second type of receivership, and one with which most PMDs will be more familiar (hopefully not by prior experience): where the bank appoints an AR (known in the past as a 'receiver and manager').*

It is this ability to appoint an AR under its floating charge which is so important to a bank, for whereas a receiver under a fixed charge has no power to manage or administer the company, an AR takes immediate effective control of the management of the company and he alone decides whether the company shall continue to trade in whole or in part and which management direction he is going to take.

Following the appointment of an AR, the management functions of the directors cease forthwith although their statutory responsibilities as directors remain. *It should by now be evident that it is only possible to follow the receivership route where the bank holds the necessary debenture and is prepared to make the necessary appointment.*

As a general rule, banks are reluctant to appoint an AR unless they see their security as being in jeopardy or are worried that they might not recover their monies in full if trading continues.

Sometimes it will be the PMD himself who requests the bank to appoint an AR, perhaps because the company is under severe creditor pressure or because he is concerned about a possible future claim against him for wrongful trading (see chapter 1), and in either event receivership appears a favourable alternative to outright liquidation.

If attempting to alleviate creditor pressure or the avoidance of personal liability are seen as negative reasons for desiring the appointment of an AR, there are a number of very positive reasons for considering receivership as a way forward.

The major benefits of receivership to an insolvent company are:

1 The bank will usually fund an AR to enable the company to continue to trade in order to achieve higher prices for the assets on the basis of a going concern; and

2 There is no automatic termination of trade for tax purposes. This means that losses in the current accounting period should be available for offset against a capital gain (arising say on a sale of the company's freehold premises) in the same period.

In a liquidation those losses would themselves be 'lost' and any capital gain would be payable without loss relief.

Under a receivership, where trading continues, these losses would be available for offset, thereby saving capital gains tax and leaving more money available for creditors generally.

3 The opportunity which an AR has to sell the company's main business activity as a going concern often helps to preserve employment for the workforce.

Receivership tended in the past to be less popular than formal liquidation with unsecured creditors (not that they had any say in the matter), because it prevented them obtaining the benefit of relief for VAT on their outstanding debts and it was generally more difficult to obtain information from a receiver than from a liquidator. However,

a Legislation which came into effect in 1986 has made it possible for an AR to issue a certificate where he believes that were the company to proceed to immediate liquidation there would be no likelihood of a dividend for unsecured creditors. Creditors may now claim VAT bad debt relief following the issue of such a certificate. (NB: The 1990 Budget proposes that VAT bad debt relief should be available automatically where a debt has been outstanding and unpaid for more than two years and has been written off in the trader's accounts.)

b Since December 1986, an AR has been obliged to convene a meeting of creditors within three months of his appointment and report to them upon specified aspects of the insolvency. As such, unsecured creditors should now be in no worse position than they would under a liquidation and could ultimately have their position improved, given the opportunity of better realisations.

Whether the appointment of an AR is at the insistence of the bank or at the request of the PMD, the AR acts as agent of the company and not of the bank – although the actual choice of appointee will almost inevitably be that of the bank. This is because banks prefer to work with ARs who are known to them and whose proven track records indicate their experience and suitability for a specific appointment.

It is customary for banks to require the PMD to write a formal letter (drafted by the bank) requesting the appointment of a named individual – usually totally unknown to the PMD – as AR. Where the PMD has approached the bank with a request that it makes an appointment, it would be difficult to refuse any requirement to confirm that request by formal letter.

However, even when the appointment is required by the bank and unwelcome to the PMD, it is likely that the bank will attempt to persuade him to send a similar letter of request. This might happen particularly when the PMD has personally guaranteed the company's overdraft. After all, if the worst happens, there is a shortfall to the bank and he is called upon under his guarantee, he can hardly turn round and blame the outcome on the bank if it has on file his letter requesting it to appoint the AR.

It is not suggested that the PMD should refuse any request by the bank to sign a formal letter requesting that it appoint an AR to his company. What he should do is to have a full discussion with the bank manager in the presence of his own professional advisers and come to a decision based upon their considered conclusions.

One positive step they might suggest (if the exercise has not already been carried out) is that the bank delay any decision for up to forty-eight hours to allow the PMD to instruct independent insolvency accountants of his own choosing to carry out an immediate financial appraisal and prepare an up-to-date statement of affairs. Although it is almost certain that the bank would still insist upon its own choice of AR, this second opinion could prove very useful to the PMD and in extreme circumstances provide a yardstick by which to monitor and perhaps even criticise any eventual AR's performance.

One argument that might be put forward against any suggestion of a second opinion is that of cost. Given that the company is already suffering a financial crisis, how can any additional and perhaps unnecessary expense be justified at such a time?

There is a very compelling counter-argument. If an AR is appointed he will immediately serve written notice on the PMD, requiring him to have sworn and returned to him within twenty-one days a full statement of affairs of the company prepared in statutory form. The letter will go on to say that he, the AR, is empowered to allow the reasonable costs involved in the preparation of this document to be met out of the assets of the company.

So, given that a statement of affairs has to be drawn up in any event and the company is going to have to meet the cost of the exercise, would it not be better to have it prepared sooner rather than later? Who knows, there might be an occasion when its immediate preparation could disclose a financial position which renders the need for any appointment unnecessary.

One thing the PMD should expect is that his independent accountants will require cleared funds *before* the conclusion of their work. It would not be appropriate for them to have to rank unsecured for their fees in any subsequent receivership, administration or liquidation. (It does happen.)

'Timing,' as King Canute was heard to remark ruefully, following his miscalculation of the turn of the tide, 'is everything'. It is no good asking the bank for days of grace when you call in at lunchtime on a Friday to cash the wages cheque. It is one thing to ask for a day or two to consider the position, quite another to require it to increase its exposure during that period.

If possible, therefore, try to ensure that any financial crisis comes to a head early in the week or towards the middle of the month, when wages and salaries are problems that follow, rather than determine, a decision!

Where the PMD has guaranteed the company's bank borrowings,

he will take a keen interest in knowing whether there is any likelihood of his having to pay anything under that guarantee. The statement of affairs should provide a guide to the likely eventual outcome of the receivership and enable him to assess any risk to his personal assets. We will consider the statement of affairs in chapter 4 of the book.

Once appointed, it is the AR's job to collect in the assets of the company and repay the debenture holder *and the company's preferential creditors*.

When we think about it, the requirement for the AR to pay the preferential creditors is quite logical. It is the charge over the assets out of which they are going to be paid – the floating charge assets – which enables him to manage the company as opposed simply to receive or recover its assets and floating charge realisations belong to the preferential creditors.

It has been known for PMDs to delay paying over the state debts – PAYE, NIC and VAT – in order to assist with cash flow and release funds to ensure continuity of trade supplies.

There are two compelling reasons for prompt payment of state debts. The first – which we will come across in due course – is that the larger the preferential creditors the smaller the chance of any surplus from the floating charge assets and the correspondingly greater possibility of a shortfall to the bank and a claim under any personal guarantee.

The second is in the context of disqualification of directors. The judgment of Sir Nicholas Browne-Wilkinson in the case of Lo-Line Electric Motors Ltd given on 30 March 1988 established that the Courts tend to hold failure by directors to discharge preferential debts as more culpable than failure to pay commercial debts. *It is in the PMD's own interests to make certain that payments of preferential debts are kept up to date.*

Questions and answers

There are so many facets involved in any receivership situation that it is impossible to deal with them all. (Receivership under an Agricultural Charge is so specialised that we are not even going to try to cover the subject.)

To most PMDs the whole concept of receivership is as much a mystery as the thought of having to go through the process is a nightmare.

In order to attempt to address some of the questions which often trouble PMDs and to remove some of the mystery surrounding receiverships, we will construct what could be a typical question-and-answer conversation between a PMD and an experienced receiver.

23

Q I've often heard the expression, 'A receiver's been appointed to so and so's company'. What does it mean?

A It usually means that a bank, having lent money to the company, has decided that it wants it back and has appointed an individual called an Administrative Receiver to recover those monies on its behalf.

Q Can a bank appoint a receiver to any company to which it has lent money?

A No. To be able to make such an appointment, it first of all has to have a debenture, duly registered at Companies House, giving the bank a charge over the assets of the company.

Q I don't like the idea at all of a receiver walking into my company. I can appreciate the bank requiring security, especially as it is lending other people's money, but would I not be better off giving security outside the company?

A Only if you don't mind putting your own personal assets at risk. The unsecured trade creditors would be very grateful to you because it means that there would be only the preferential creditors to rank before them in any insolvency. Your family might have other things to say about you.

Remember that you are only ever likely to hear talk of a receiver if your company is insolvent. Under these circumstances would you rather that the bank was paid out of the company's assets than out of your own pocket?

Q Suppose the bank has a debenture over my company's assets and trade is not too good. Are there any warning signs that could indicate that the bank is looking at my company with a view to appointing a receiver?

A We'll be talking about one such warning sign in chapter 4 – the requirement by the bank for the company to open a Wages Account. Another sign would be a request by the bank for additional security, particularly when this is to support existing borrowings rather than an increase in facility.

Should you receive a request for additional security, particularly when it is of a personal, collateral nature, be certain to discuss the overall implications with your solicitor and financial adviser.

Q I suppose that requests to open a wages account and for additional security must be regarded as early warning signs. Is anything else likely to happen before an unwelcome AR walks through the door?

A Yes indeed. Your bank is most unlikely to appoint an unwelcome receiver without being certain that your company is in severe financial trouble and its money is at risk. It will almost certainly require up-to-date financial information and it will normally require the company formally to instruct in writing – and pay in advance – independent insolvency accountants who will, at short notice, visit your premises. They will go through your books and records, ask you a lot of questions, and deliver to you and the bank a written report which will incorporate an up-to-date statement of affairs and their recommendations upon how the bank should proceed.

One further point: if your letter of instruction is asked to name a specific partner in the firm of accountants to carry out the investigation, then you will know the identity of the bank's choice of AR in advance.

Q I can take it then that once these 'independent accountants' get their foot in the door my business is as good as finished. After all, they're certain to slant the report in such a way as to secure an appointment, aren't they?

A That's a very cynical and fortunately generally unfounded worry. It is true that such complaints have been heard in isolated instances in past years, but, overall, a great deal of integrity is involved and banks have developed a very high degree of sophistication in assessing the true position, irrespective of anyone else's conclusions.

Many a business has been saved following such an investigation. Remember that these accountants know nothing of your business before they walk in and they are often able to give objective advice which, when acted upon, can restore profitability.

Q Even if I accept what you say, there is an exception to every rule and with my luck I am certain to get an accountant who either because he is incompetent, short of work, or simply having a bad day, will write an unfair report that will put me out of business. How can I guard against that?

A If you have any doubts at all, you should ask your own financial advisers to recommend to you an insolvency accountant whom they know personally and in whom they have undoubted trust. You then ask the bank manager if he would be prepared to allow this accountant to carry out the independent appraisal.

Now you have to remember, just as you fear that the bank's chosen expert might bias his report against you, the bank will be equally concerned that anyone you choose will not be totally objective, so that it is unlikely to agree.

However, there might just be a chance that the accountant recommended to you is also well known to the bank and, indeed, forms one of a handful of accountants whom it instructs from time to time to carry out the very kind of appraisal in question. Given that the bank has implicit trust in this man's integrity, then there is just an outside chance that it might make an exception to its rule and allow your own choice of reporting accountant.

Q That might happen for others, it's never going to happen for me! Now what do I do?

A You tell the bank that whilst acceding to its very understandable and proper request, you are going to adopt a 'two heads are better than one' principle and the company is going to instruct and pay for its own independent expert to work alongside the bank's choice. If the worst comes to the worst and the bank's fears are realised, then the statutory statement of affairs  which you will be required to produce following the appointment of an AR will have already been compiled in draft form by 'your' expert and his time involvement will not have been wasted.

If the experts disagree, then the bank will require them to reconcile their differences and, failing this, will almost certainly proceed down the route recommended by its own expert. Should this happen, then you will at least have your own expert's report on file, which can always be used in evidence should you be dissatisfied with the eventual outcome of the receivership. *I want to stress, however, that we are talking about isolated instances.* Under normal circumstances you will be able to rely upon the bank to choose an independent expert who knows exactly what to do and how to do it.

Q What is likely to happen if, unknown to me, the bank has decided to appoint a receiver without going through the stage of having a report compiled? How will I know to prepare for a receiver's knock on the door?

A The bank will serve formal demand upon you in writing requesting that you pay to it all monies due, including interest, as at the date of the demand. The actual amount required will be stated.

This demand will normally be served upon the company personally by the bank's messenger. Once you receive the letter of demand, you will know that the receiver is on his way.

Q How long will I be given to find the required funds in order to prevent the receivership?

A Not long at all. You must realise that the bank will only serve notice upon you after all other avenues of refinancing have been explored. In reality you will already have tried and failed to borrow money elsewhere and once the decision to appoint has been taken the machinery moves very quickly.

In practice, the receiver will have been chosen a day or so before. The paperwork will have been all drawn up and in place either before or at the same time as the issue of demand for repayment. If the receiver-elect is from out of town it is likely that he will have travelled to within close proximity of your premises and, to exaggerate but slightly, his car engine will already be ticking over.

It will usually be within two or three hours that the receiver will arrive and in some cases could be even sooner. There is no set time between the demand and the appointment: the court held in one instance, where demands were served on two associated companies at 9.45 a.m. and between 10.00 a.m. and 10.15 a.m. respectively and the receivers were appointed just after 11.00 a.m. the same morning, that the time intervals were quite sufficient.

Q So, I have received my demand, I have not repaid the bank and the receiver is standing outside the front door with his team of followers. Is it in order for me to hide them away in an obscure corner of the building to do whatever they have to do and get on with running my own business?

A Sorry; it doesn't work like that at all. If anyone is likely to be placed in an obscure corner of the building or even dismissed and sent home, it is going to be you: that is, if you attempt to obstruct the receiver from carrying out his duties or fail to co-operate fully with him in running the business – which incidentally is, to all intents and purposes, no longer yours.

Q It sounds worse than I thought. You had better tell me a bit more about it. What will happen when the receiver walks into my business?

A The first thing you will need to come to terms with is the dreadful feeling of humiliation. Whether it is your bad management or outside economic forces that have caused the problem, the simple truth is that your business has failed and now you have to stand on one side and watch someone else take control of what you very likely regard as your 'baby'.

It is to be hoped that your receiver will be one of the kind and understanding breed and not the jack-booted type we have all read about and secretly dread should ever have the opportunity of crossing our portals.

Nevertheless, although kindness and understanding in a receiver can be very helpful and comforting, you have to realise that, however unpleasant his task, he has a job to do and he will do it irrespective of your wishes. The best thing you can do is to place all your expertise and contacts at his disposal to enable him, assisted by such agents as he appoints, to obtain the most advantageous realisation of the company's assets, thereby improving the chances of paying not just the bank, but perhaps all other creditors and, even if he is not able to save the business in its present form, afford the opportunity of salvaging the main trading activity and preserving employment for some of the workforce.

Q I seem to remember having read earlier that the receiver effectively takes over the management of the company and decides which direction the business will take. Does this mean that he will continue to run the business until he is able to sell it and, if so, will I have the opportunity to buy it?

A Let us try to take one thing at a time. The first task of the receiver will be to appraise the company's overall position. What has caused the insolvency? Are all or some parts of the business capable of profitable trading? Should it be shut down immediately to preserve further losses? Can he justify borrowing still further money from the bank to pay wages and overheads to allow him to continue to trade in the hopes of securing a better price for the assets by selling them, along with the goodwill of the business, as a going concern?

He has to address these and many other points before he can come to any decisions, and you will begin to understand how important was that initial appraisal which he carried out and which allowed him to report to the bank before his appointment. It will have given him a feel for the business and enabled him to draw certain conclusions and determine the future course of the receivership with a minimum of delay. This is extremely important; the first few days in a receivership are a hiatus period and the decisions required are hard enough in themselves, but imagine the working atmosphere in which they have to be carried out. You, the PMD, will be in a state of shock and incapable of rational decisions. The workforce will be desperately troubled as to whether they face redundancy and, at a time when working efficiently has never been more important, they will be seeking assurances the receiver has no power to give and holding meetings amongst themselves, whether officially or unofficially, to consider their plight. If all this were not enough, news of the AR's appointment will have spread through the trade like wildfire and the telephones will be ringing constantly with certain creditors enquiring as to the position concerning their outstanding accounts, whilst other creditors will be turning up on the doorstep demanding return of their unpaid goods over which they claim a reservation of title.

Meanwhile, creditors who are already owed money have to be charmed into maintaining a continuity of supply; security has to be in place; locks sometimes changed; circulars prepared for debtors and creditors; the old trading records to be completed up to the date of appointment and new ledgers opened; computers have to be understood and perhaps reprogrammed.

The receiver and his men have to deal with all this and much more; they call it 'fire-fighting' and it is in this atmosphere that cool judgment has to be exercised and important decisions reached.

Q You are beginning to make me feel sorrier for the receiver than I do for myself! You haven't, however, answered the second part of my previous question: will I have the opportunity of buying the business from the receiver?

A Anything is possible. If you can persuade outside backers – do not waste your time approaching the company's current bankers who have appointed the AR – that despite the receivership you have, either alone or with others, the management expertise to run a future profitable, perhaps streamlined, operation then, provided you offer more money than anyone else, an effective management buy-out might be feasible.

Q I am beginning to think that perhaps receivership might not be so bad after all. What would you say to that?

A Let us be under no illusion, receivership is a traumatic experience which every PMD would do best to avoid whenever possible – a view shared by the banks.

Although it is usually far preferable to an immediate liquidation in that it affords at least the opportunity of saving the company and the jobs of the workforce, it is still the beginning of the end for many a PMD. Even where the AR is able to sell part of the business, it is likely that in the majority of cases there will be no permanent position offered to the PMD – and, don't forget, there are others besides yourself who are going to suffer. There are creditors, some of whose own futures might hang in the balance if they are not to be paid.

Q You are absolutely right – I was forgetting the creditors. What will happen to them and is there anything that I could do to help?

A Creditors (other than the debenture holder) who are secured on specific assets of the company, for example motor vehicles on hire-purchase, will immediately seek to recover their security from the receiver, sell it at the best possible price and will either hand over any surplus to the receiver or submit a claim for any shortfall to rank unsecured. Where there are a number of hire-purchase agreements with the same finance company, you can usually expect a consolidation clause to be in operation and the hire-purchase company will look to the combined sale proceeds of all the assets covered by those agreements to be available against the combined borrowings under the agreements.

The preferential creditors will be dealt with by the receiver and it is unlikely, even if they were in the process of attempting to recover monies, that they will continue with any further action against the company. Their classification as preferential means exactly what it says: their claims will be met out of the available assets of the company before any payments can be made to the general body of unsecured creditors.

Apart from the shareholders, it is the unsecured creditors whose claims are most at risk. You ask if there is anything you can do to help; you can start by complying with the receiver's demand for a statement of affairs, which will enable him to assess dividend prospects for the unsecured creditors. If the position is hopeless and no dividend would be likely were the company to proceed to immediate liquidation, then the receiver is allowed to issue a certificate to that effect and advise each creditor that this has been done. (He will not send them a copy of the certificate – simply notify them that it has been issued.) As soon as they receive that notification from the receiver, the unsecured creditors are able to claim any appropriate element of VAT bad debt relief. An effective reduction of 15 per cent of their claims may not seem large, but it has been known to buy individual creditors time to stave off their own insolvency following the 'domino effect'.

If there is going to be no dividend for unsecured creditors,

then you might consider that there is no point in placing the company into subsequent liquidation now that they are able to obtain their VAT bad debt relief under the circumstances already outlined. (At one time this relief was available only if the company went into liquidation.) Individual creditors may, of course, hold a totally different view – something we will consider in a moment – but they will at least be able to attend and air their views at the meeting of creditors which the AR is now obliged to hold within three months following his appointment.

The position is far more complicated where there is every chance that a reasonable dividend might ultimately be available for the unsecured creditors once the receiver has finished his work and the bank and preferential creditors paid in full. It is not easy to spell this out, but let us try to keep it as simple as possible.

There is no way of saying how long the receiver will continue to run the company. No receiver likes to remain 'in harness' a moment longer than is necessary. He will want either to sell the business or close it down and dispose of the assets piecemeal at the earliest opportunity. On the other hand, it is going to be a considerable period of time before the Inland Revenue and the Customs and Excise are able to submit and the receiver agree their final preferential claims and, until this has been done, the receiver will be unable to part with any monies which might remain after he has paid the debenture holder in full.

What we have then is the receiver dealing with the claims of the debenture holder and the preferential creditors and the general body of unsecured creditors left in limbo, as it were, with no one to protect their interests. It is true that any creditors' committee formed at the one statutory meeting of creditors to be held within three months of the AR's appointment, has the right to demand information from the receiver, but the likelihood of any information filtering through to the general body of unsecured creditors is remote.

It is because of this that creditors will usually prefer to see the company go into liquidation sooner, rather than later. This may not suit the receiver at all. First of all, his actual legal status changes subtly to his detriment immediately the company is liquidated. This need not concern the PMD and neither does it necessarily have any practical effect upon any eventual outcome for creditors. It is, however, important to the AR himself, who may well, quite understandably, attempt to resist any suggestions of an early liquidation.

There are occasions when it would be totally against the interests of unsecured creditors for the company to proceed to liquidation until a certain stage of the receivership has been attained. The obvious example that springs to mind is where the receiver is hoping to sell either the business or certain of its major assets at a price which will create substantial gains over book values. Liquidation brings with it an automatic cessation of trade for taxation purposes and there could well be losses available in the company which the receiver could have utilised to offset any gain, thereby reducing or even expunging a capital gains tax liability.

You will see then that if you are to do all you can for the unsecured creditors, you should:

1 Fulfil your statutory requirement to furnish the AR with a full statement of affairs of the company within twenty-one days of his appointment.
2 Try to ascertain from discussions with the receiver whether it is likely there might be an eventual surplus after his own costs and after he has paid the debenture holder and the preferential creditors in full.
3 If there is to be a surplus:
a find out whether the receiver could be frustrated in his efforts to maximise realisations if the company were to be placed into liquidation; and
b try to agree a time-scale with the AR for convening a formal meeting of the company's creditors in order that they may appoint their choice of liquidator. (This would be

immediately following a meeting of shareholders held to place the company into liquidation.)

4 If any of the company's creditors attempt to place the company into liquidation and you know, following your discussions with the receiver, that should this happen it could create an unnecessary taxation liability upon the receiver's sale of the assets, attempt to explain to the creditor that if he continues with his action he could well harm his own interests, and undertake to place the company into liquidation as soon as the receiver's objective has been achieved.

Q You were right about its not being easy. I hope I understand most of what you have said, but you have lost me when you start talking about liquidation and receivership at the same time, and how can creditors put the company into liquidation once a receiver has been appointed?

A I can understand your confusion. Remember that the receiver acts only for the debenture holder and the preferential creditors. A *liquidator acts for all creditors* and the appointment of a receiver does not prevent the appointment of a liquidator.

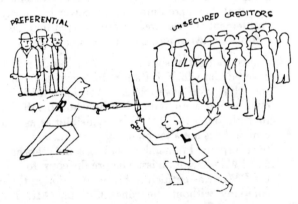

Conversely, the appointment of a liquidator would not prevent the debenture holder from appointing their own receiver and banks have, on occasion, been known to appoint a receiver to safeguard the assets under their charge upon learning that the company had gone into liquidation and that the liquidator is either unknown to them or, for whatever reason, they believe that they have a chance of better recovery if they make their own appointment.

Where the bank has not appointed an AR and the company goes into liquidation, the liquidator would have the right to handle and dispose of the assets covered by the debenture holder, subject to its approval and accounting to it for the proceeds of sale, less any costs he is able to persuade it to authorise.

Where the company is in liquidation and the bank subsequently appoints a receiver, the liquidator must effectively withdraw leaving the receiver to handle all the assets of the company. The only work of a practical nature that the liquidator can then undertake is to attempt to agree the claims of the unsecured creditors. Even this can sometimes prove difficult for, although it is the liquidator who has the legal right to possession of the company's books and records, the receiver is entitled to have full access to them and will almost inevitably hold them in the normal course of his duties.

The ultimate weapon available to an unsecured creditor (outside of somehow being able to convert his status to that of a secured creditor) is to use his unsatisfied claim to bring about the compulsory winding-up of the company. We are going to talk about this again – but not here. That is, except to say, that the appointment of a receiver in no way affects the entitlement of unsecured creditors to petition the court for the compulsory winding-up of the company.

Q I have thought of something which you do not seem to have covered and which, if I am right, seems to be in conflict with something you have told me. You have said, in effect, that once an AR is appointed it is he who runs the company and that although the PMD's responsibilities as a director still remain he is not allowed to deal with the assets or business of the company. I remember reading some years ago that an AR and PMD fought an issue before the court to decide whether the PMD was entitled to bring an action in the name of the company without the consent of the AR. I recall being interested at the time, for the proposition seemed to me outrageous that a receiver could abandon or not pursue an asset to the detriment of the PMD bank guarantor, and I was delighted when I saw that the PMD had won the case. Does my memory serve me right?

A Indeed it does, but please be very careful! You must, I think, be referring to the case of *Newhart* v. *Co-operative Commercial Bank Ltd*. This was, however, a very special case in that the 'asset' the receiver chose to ignore was an action for damages by the company against the debenture holder. It was only because the action for damages was not an asset that the receiver had 'taken into his possession or control' that the court decided the board was therefore free (and under a duty) to bring the action in the interests of unsecured creditors and shareholders.

You will, then, realise that this in no way creates a charter for directors to interfere in a receivership and the instances when such action by a PMD might be appropriate are few and far between. If you ever come across the situation, be certain to talk it through with your legal adviser before making any rash moves.

Q I know you have advised that I should co-operate with the AR, but I have heard of some frightening experiences suffered by a PMD following the appointment of an AR to his company.

Given the strength of the AR's legal position, what should the PMD do if he finds himself with an AR whom he mistrusts and with whom he cannot work?

A He must be guided by his solicitor at the time. This does happen from time to time, but no fixed formula can apply. Whatever happens, do not be deliberately obstructive to the AR – this can only backfire if the receivership turns out to be a disaster. I suppose all I can say is, do your best to be as helpful as possible, whilst at the same time protecting your own position by consulting your solicitor.

Q We have talked throughout of fixed and floating charges and debenture holders as if these expressions were unique to banks. I know for certain that one of my business colleagues, who had never in his life owed money to the bank, had a receiver appointed to his business, so am I right in thinking that it isn't just banks that are able to take this type of security and, following from this, appoint a receiver?

A You are absolutely right. If you recall, we said right at the beginning of this section that anyone lending money to a company could require that security be given to safeguard their advance. To demonstrate the extreme to which this proposition can apply, consider the famous case of the cobbler who, having traded successfully for many years as a sole trader (pun not intended!) decided to incorporate a company to assume his business and thereafter allow him to trade with the benefit of limited liability.

The cobbler decided that he would not take shares in the new company equal to the net capital which was employed in his business. He took instead a mere handful of shares, leaving the rest of his capital standing to his credit in the company as a director's loan. He decided, however, that he was not going to rank unsecured as regards his loan and, acting in his capacity as a director of the company, granted to himself, as an individual, a debenture over his loan capital and duly registered his charge at Companies House.

Subsequently, his company became insolvent and went into liquidation and the validity of his debenture was challenged before the court. The judge had no hesitation in upholding the PMD cobbler's right to payment of his loan from the proceeds of the charged assets even though his trade creditors were to receive nothing. The reasoning is simple enough: the whole purpose of registering the charge at Companies House is to place that information on public record and it is open and available for any trade creditor to have that record searched before agreeing to extend credit to the company. In other words, a supplier can assess his risk before he decides to give credit and anyone lending money to a company where its main director feels the need to charge the company's entire assets to give priority to his own advances, ought to have more sense.

When you come across the expression 'receivership' it is more than likely to be a bank appointment. There are, however, certain trades where money is lent by a supplier to a customer in order to tie that customer to the supplier as regards future purchases. One example that springs to mind is the brewing industry, and it is quite possible that your friend was the landlord of a so-called free house and had borrowed a large sum of money at advantageous rates of interest from a specific brewery. As consideration for the loan, he will have given a debenture to the brewery and agreed to purchase its products, either exclusively or to a certain minimum level, during such time as any part of the loan remains outstanding. Such an arrangement is of obvious benefit to both sides, the brewery enjoying profits from future assured sales, the landlord paying less interest on the loan than he would have paid to a bank had he gone to it instead for the funds.

Q It seems to me that this ability to grant fixed and floating charges and then simply have them registered at Companies House might be an excellent way for – dare I say it – unscrupulous individuals to gain an unfair advantage over other creditors where there is potential insolvency.

A It must be admitted that it has happened in the past but you have to differentiate between morally unfair and legally unfair. There is, moreover, a built-in legal safeguard, but it is complicated and if you suspect that anyone is trying to take charges to their own unfair advantage, you will need immediate legal advice.

In general terms, where a floating charge is granted for past consideration – that is, when the charge is taken to cover a debt already due *and the company was insolvent at the time the charge was given* – a period of twelve months must elapse before the charge becomes valid and should the company go into liquidation during that time the charge would be void against the liquidator.

If the charge is granted to a connected person, then, under the circumstances described, the time-scale would be extended to two years.

We will be discussing in chapter 4 something which is known as 'the rule in Clayton's Case', which seems to work against a bank when it comes to calculating its preferential wages claim. That same rule can work the other way when it comes to floating charges and it may well be that a bank would not have to wait a full twelve months for a floating charge to become effective, even where the overdraft was in existence when the charge was granted. Very simply, this is because the turnover on the account – that is, monies paid in to the credit of the account and then re-advanced by way of cheques, etc. drawn on the account – is deemed to comprise fresh advances and it does not take long for the entire overdraft facility to turn over, after which the charge will be deemed to have been given, not against the original overdraft, but against the 'new' overdraft of equal amount, and will be valid.

The position concerning fixed charges granted other than for new borrowings is somewhat different. Here we are concerned with time-scales ranging from six months up to (in the case of transactions of an undervalue, or transactions with connected persons) two years. Such charges could be invalid if they formed what is known as a preference – that is they placed the recipient in a better position over other creditors at a time when the company either was insolvent, or becomes insolvent by virtue of the preference itself.

The relevant provisions that govern the invalidity of floating charges and (voidable) preferences might affect the position of an AR if the company goes into insolvent liquidation. (Insolvent liquidation means any liquidation other than a members' voluntary liquidation where creditors will be paid in full within twelve months.)

It is because of these provisions that we sometimes hear of unsecured creditors petitioning to wind up a company where they suspect preferences have been made or charges have been given to others which could be set aside if dealt with in time, for once the relevant period has passed, i.e. six months to two years, depending upon the circumstances, the preferences cannot be attacked and the charges become valid and binding.

Were it not for this minimum six-month period, creditors would need to carry out monthly searches of the register at Companies House to find out whether charges had been granted which might jeopardise their chances of being paid. As it is, a regular search on a half-yearly basis would be a prudent precaution – particularly where substantial amounts are at risk.

Q You have been good enough to repeat all of that three times, the last time very slowly, and I still find it most confusing. I wonder if we can just try to précis what you have said. Am I correct in saying:

a That no AR can seek to set aside a floating or fixed charge and that, wearing my hat as an unsecured creditor rather than a PMD, if a Receiver were appointed to a company that owed me money and I learned that charges had been given or assets transferred to other creditors or associates during the last two years – and particularly during the last six months – I should attempt to have the company wound up compulsorily; and

b Whereas the only way I would know if assets had been given and physically removed, as opposed to legally charged, was if someone told me or I found out by accident, a search at Companies House would tell me immediately if any attempt had been made to charge the company's assets to someone else?

A You are basically correct, but discuss the relevant facts with your solicitor at the time. An AR can be affected by, rather than himself affect, charges or preferences. This is because he has no powers to challenge their validity, so that creditors may be obliged to seek an early liquidation in order to crystallise and preserve the maximum preference period. (Incidentally, an administrator, unlike an AR, can also challenge charges and preferences.)

So far as searching the register of charges on the company's file at Companies House is concerned, this is something you would normally ask your accountant or solicitor to arrange for you. It can take a week or so for this information to appear on file, so that if you are at all suspicious, check again in about six weeks' time.

Q I can see that if there is going to be nothing for unsecured creditors, the company will either go into liquidation or simply lie dormant and eventually be struck off the register. What is the position where it seems possible that a dividend will be available for unsecured creditors; does the company still have to go into liquidation once the receiver has withdrawn?

A In theory, no; in practice, not necessarily but usually.

If the receiver has disposed of the company's assets all that will be left is cash in hand and there would seem to be little point in attempting to save the company. The object of the exercise in such a case would be to divide that cash among the unsecured creditors, by way of a dividend upon their claims, as quickly as possible.

If the receiver has managed to realise sufficient assets to discharge the debenture holder and the preferential creditors in full and there still remains a central core of the business which continues to trade, then there may well be every good reason for trying to strike some compromise deal with the unsecured creditors which would afford the company an opportunity of continuing. In other words, if the creditors would accept a percentage of their claims, the monies saved, which were otherwise shown in the balance sheet as owing to creditors, could be used to re-capitalise the business by counter-balancing previous losses.

There are now two formal schemes available, one of which could be adopted in an attempt to save such a company from final liquidation. These schemes are the two branch roads which we mentioned at the beginning of this chapter, namely:

1 A Scheme under Section 425 of the Companies Act 1985; or

2 A Company Voluntary Arrangement (under Part 1 of the Insolvency Act 1986).

Q I have just looked back at the diagram at the beginning of chapter 2 and I see there that you showed these branch roads as being branches from the main route of administration orders and not of receivership. Are you telling me now it is the other way round?

A Certainly not. As you will come to see in due course they will more usually be found flowing from an administration order than from a receivership. They are not, however, exclusive to either route; indeed, were it not for certain difficulties we would see them far more often as a way forward in their own right.

Q Please describe them to me – what are they and when would you use them?

A All in good time. Just as we have had to deal with a great many insolvency topics under this receivership section, so it is more convenient for us to deal with these branch roads when we come to talk about administration orders.

Q You've given me a new idea. You have said that receivership will usually be preferable to immediate liquidation but now you have mentioned an administration order. Is it possible for a company that has granted a debenture to a bank to have an administration order made in its favour as an alternative to the bank's appointing a receiver, and would this be better for the PMD?

A It is possible that an administrator could be appointed to do the job of an AR, but only if the debenture holder agrees. I suspect that any PMD would prefer the thought of an administrator to an AR and there is one immediate positive advantage to the company. We have learned that the appointment of an AR does not act as a bar to any creditor pursuing his claim to the extent of obtaining a winding up order against the company, placing it into compulsory liquidation. When an administrator is appointed under an administration order all rights of action against the company are suspended, so that the company is safe from the threat of compulsory liquidation until such time as the administration order is discharged.

Q I think I like the sound of an administration order better than the thought of a receivership. Can you tell me more about it?

A Certainly. Read the next section.

Administration Order

Until 29 December 1986, the date of the implementation of the Insolvency Act 1986, it was almost impossible for an insolvent company to be able to trade – even given the consent of its secured creditors – outside of a formal receivership. This was because unsecured creditors had to agree not to press for their claims, which would then effectively be frozen, allowing the company, as it were, to start again, leaving the current burden of debt to be paid as and when profitability was restored.

Quite apart from the difficulty in arranging new finance to re-capitalise the company, any informal arrangement of this nature – known as a moratorium – required the agreement of *every* individual creditor and this was, in most cases, impossible to obtain.

It was because of this that a company which had not granted a debenture to its bankers, or whose bankers, for whatever reason, were reluctant to appoint a receiver (in those days called a 'receiver and manager'), was almost inevitably forced into liquidation.

Section 425 scheme

To be strictly honest there was an alternative – at least in theory – which still remains with us following the 1986 insolvency legislation, and that is the opportunity to attempt a scheme under Section 425 of the Companies Act 1985 (previously Section 206 of the Companies Act 1948). The scheme in question would be an attempt to reconstruct the company and, in its simplest form, could be restricted to trying to per-suade the unsecured creditors to accept an agreed percentage of their debt in full and final settlement of their claims.

The advantage of succeeding with a Section 425 scheme is that even if one or more creditor refuses point blank to agree, the court will bind them to the arrangement provided the necessary assents required by the Act have been achieved.

The required assents are a simple majority (i.e. more than 50 per cent) of creditors present, either personally or by proxy, at a meeting convened for voting purposes, whose combined claims in value must amount to at least 75 per cent of the total claims of all creditors.

The problems in taking a Section 425 scheme through to a satis-factory conclusion are a mixture of practicability and simple logistics: who is going to provide on-going finance to an insolvent company and how are you going to put the scheme together and take it through to a satisfactory conclusion before one creditor obtains a winding-up order against the company or converts a judgment debt into a charge on the company's assets? (Remember our advice to creditors: 'thrice blest he who gets his blow in fust!')

The first of the problems should be reasonably self-explanatory; the logistical problem becomes more apparent when we look at what is actually involved in attempting a 425 scheme.

Where such a compromise is proposed, the court may order that a meeting (in our case, of the creditors) be summoned to consider and vote upon the scheme.

In practice, this will inevitably mean that two meetings will have to be held, as no one is going to go to the very considerable trouble and expense of attempting a scheme that has little or no chance of success. This means that an earlier meeting will be needed to sound out the feeling of the creditors – something which the court will take into account when deciding whether or not the formal meeting should be summoned for voting purposes.

Neither the creditors nor the court will be impressed if they are simply told that the company is insolvent and that the directors hope to be able to come up with proposals to save the company. Everyone needs to know what those proposals are, how the scheme is to operate and when and how much he is likely to be paid.

Professional advisers will need to be involved, who will only put their names to any proposed scheme if they have the fullest financial information and have had an opportunity to study the precise state of the company's affairs. This will inevitably mean a full investigation and the preparation of a report which will include a Statement of Affairs.

All of this takes time – something which any company in financial difficulty simply does not have. It is because of this that schemes under Section 425 of the Companies Act 1985 tend only to be used as ways forward in their own right in special circumstances, where companies – often quite large concerns – are wanting to reconstruct the basis of their share capital (that is, amend the rights of shareholders as opposed to compromise with their creditors), and a formal scheme is needed to bind a dissenting minority.

(The only other available formal statutory procedures were to be found under Section 582 or 601 of the Companies Act 1985. These would have been of no use to any PMD attempting a compromise with his creditors and mention is made simply to cover the subject in its entirety.)

Company voluntary arrangement

Since the introduction of the new legislation contained in the Insolvency Act 1986, a new, simplified scheme has been introduced which is known as a Company Voluntary Arrangement (CVA). Here again, however, it seems as if this route will more normally be a branch road of one of the three main routes forward, namely, receivership, administration order or liquidation.

It might appear strange at first sight that a liquidation should or could be converted into a CVA, or that any liquidator could – or even would want to – apply to the court to seek a voluntary arrangement. It is not likely to happen very often, but circumstances do sometimes

45

change and this option now affords the opportunity of halting any winding-up.

Suppose, for example, that a patent held by the company, hitherto believed to be of indifferent value, was suddenly found after liquidation to be worth a great deal. The liquidator could (by virtue of Section 1(3)(b) of the Insolvency Act 1986) apply to the company and its creditors with a view to seeking a voluntary arrangement as a first step towards restoring the company to a trading position.

It will, then, be only in exceptional instances that we come across a liquidator seeking a CVA. More normally it will be an administrator or the directors who begin by making a proposal to the company and its creditors (under Part 1 of the Insolvency Act 1986), but:

1 any proposed scheme cannot be made binding upon the *secured* creditors without their consent; and

2 there is nothing to prevent creditors from taking action against the company while the proposals for the voluntary arrangement are being drawn up and considered.

These two criteria are sufficient in themselves to limit the likely utilisation of CVAs as anything other than a branch road, but there is a further factor which could come into play and which we will describe as the:

3 '15 per cent VAT penalty'.

It is possible under certain circumstances in administrative receiverships and administration orders for creditors to obtain bad debt relief on the VAT element of their claims. (We have discussed those circumstances in paragraph (a) on page 20.)

Such relief is not allowable, however, where a company proceeds directly to the route of a Section 425 scheme or a voluntary arrangement. Thus it would seem to be in creditors' interests for the company always to seek an administration order if there is any chance that either of the branch routes might ultimately prove to be the eventual way forward, and where there would be no initial likelihood of dividend prospects in an immediate liquidation.

Just as a scheme under Section 425 requires the approval of the court, so a CVA follows the submission of a report to the court by a nominee, being the individual chosen to administer the proposed CVA and who must be an authorised insolvency practitioner.

It is necessary, first of all, for the directors to prepare their own report to be delivered to the nominee, which must contain certain specific information: for example, details of the company's assets, charges and liabilities; and full details of any transactions which the company has entered into and which are capable of being challenged or set aside by a liquidator, e.g. transactions at undervalue, preferences, extortionate credit transactions or invalid floating charges. (See Sections 238, 239, 244 and 245 of the Insolvency Act 1986.)

The nominee will need details of any transactions caught by these sections which could be challenged by a liquidator because, unless directors' proposals also include their suggestions as to how these matters are to be put right, it would be improper for him to accept nomination and the company should instead proceed to liquidation.

There are many other matters which the directors' proposals must contain and within seven days after delivery of their proposals to the nominee, the directors should also deliver a full statement of the company's affairs, duly certified as correct, made up to a date not earlier than two weeks before the date of the notice to the nominee.

Within 28 days of receiving the proposals, the nominee must add to them his own report, which must be submitted to the court, in which he will be required to express an opinion as to whether members (i.e. shareholders) and creditors should be summoned to consider the proposals and suggest suitable times and venues.

Assuming that the court gives the necessary direction, the meetings of the members and creditors can take place. For the scheme of CVA to be accepted, a majority of more than 50 per cent of the members present in person or by proxy and voting in favour of the resolution must be obtained. In the case of the creditors' meeting, a majority in excess of 75 per cent in value of the creditors present or by proxy and voting on the resolution must be obtained.

Once the CVA has been approved and accepted, the nominee becomes the supervisor of the scheme.

The Administration Order procedure
The Administration Order procedure is a novel concept in English law, introduced in Part II of the Insolvency Act 1986.

It recognises and fills the need to allow an insolvent company to continue to trade under the supervision of an administrator, to act not just for certain creditors or class of creditors, but for all creditors, though recognising the special status of any secured or preferential creditors.

47

Where receivership is impossible through lack of the necessary debenture, it affords an insolvent company the opportunity of continuing to trade under the direction of an administrator.

The appointment of an administrator is by the court upon the formal application of the company or its directors, or by a creditor. Such appointment, if granted, is not intended as a long-term solution, and an insight into the thinking of those drafting the legislation may be glimpsed by looking at the four criteria, at least one of which

must be put forward to the court as a reason for requesting an appointment, namely:

1 The likelihood of saving the main business activity of the company either wholly or in part; or
2 To facilitate a Voluntary Arrangement; or
3 To facilitate a scheme under Section 425, Companies Act 1985; or
4 The likelihood of more beneficial realisations of the assets than in a liquidation.

Here, then, we can see from 2 and 3 above that the drafters of the legislation clearly recognised the need to have some formal arrangement available to afford an insolvent company the time necessary to prepare a Section 425 scheme, or proposals for a voluntary arrangement and during which period any action by creditors was stayed. *The administration order procedure affords the company the opportunity of obtaining a formal moratorium, during which period the administrator is able to prepare proposals that might include salvaging the whole or part of the business, without the danger of creditors' placing the company into compulsory liquidation.*

It is particularly useful where no debenture has been granted, and the directors are unable to request the appointment of a receiver.

It is unlikely, although not impossible, that a company which has granted fixed and floating charges to a debenture holder will obtain an administration order as opposed to an AR being appointed, but this could happen where the debenture holder agrees to allow the assets subject to its charges to be handled by an administrator.

As already discussed, it is possible for a company that is subject to an administration order to enter into a Section 425 scheme or a CVA once the administration order has been discharged. In practice, we are more likely to see a CVA route chosen as it is simpler to operate than a scheme under Section 425 of the Companies Act 1985.

Whatever happens, an administration order is not meant to be a long-term solution, and if the company remains insolvent once the order comes to an end then, unless one of the formal schemes described is entered into, the company must inevitably proceed to liquidation.

Whether that liquidation is a compulsory liquidation or a creditors' voluntary liquidation will depend upon a number of factors. One very important consideration is the position of the preferential creditors. If the company proceeds to *compulsory* liquidation, then the relevant date for purpose of calculating preferential claims is deemed to be the date of the making of the administration order – a factor that can make a marked difference to recovery prospects.

It is because of this that if the creditors' voluntary liquidation route is preferable overall (for example to save additional costs), it is sometimes necessary for the unsecured creditors to agree to restore the position of the preferential creditors by making up any difference to them as a first payment out of the available assets.

Liquidation

The third main route, liquidation, will probably be the one best known to most Poor Man directors. It is, of course, the final solution from which there is, almost without exception, no return.

The only formal liquidation which gives comfort to anyone is members' voluntary liquidation, already discussed, where all are to be paid in full.

Liquidation is the route which every insolvent company must inevitably follow if none of the alternative routes is available. In England, there are two distinct types of insolvent liquidation, namely:

1 Creditors' Voluntary Liquidation; and
2 Compulsory Liquidation.

Creditors' voluntary liquidation

Here, the shareholders pass a resolution that the company shall be wound up and appoint a licensed insolvency practitioner of their

49

choice to be liquidator of the company. Usually later that day (but at the latest within fourteen days), a meeting of the company's creditors, duly convened, takes place for the purpose of appointing the creditors' choice of liquidator – who may or may not be the liquidator chosen by the members.

In practice, it is usual for a report to be given to the creditors by the members' nominated liquidator which will detail the history of the company leading up to the position of insolvency. It is also usual for the creditors to question the directors and it is not unknown for these meetings on occasion to become quite spirited!

In the event, the choice of liquidator is determined by a simple majority of the creditors, not in number but by value of their claims.

We will look in greater detail at meetings of creditors in chapter 4 of the book.

Compulsory liquidation

A compulsory liquidation is the outcome of a Winding-up Order being made by the court following a petition, usually by a creditor in respect of an unsatisfied claim.

The threat of a winding-up petition is a very useful weapon in the unsecured creditor's armoury. Contrary to popular conception, it is not even necessary for a creditor to have an unsatisfied judgment debt in order to petition the court. Section 123 of the Insolvency Act 1986 allows any creditor with an outstanding overdue debt (currently exceeding £750) to issue a formal demand for payment and to use the demand as evidence upon which to base a petition for a compulsory winding-up of the debtor company if it remains unsatisfied thereafter for a period of three weeks. (A word of warning: before rushing off to issue a petition, our PMD should first read the section in chapter 5 on the petition that backfired).

Occasionally, a petition for compulsory winding-up will be made by a creditor following a meeting of creditors which had originally been convened to ratify a creditors' voluntary winding-up. This would normally happen as a result of the creditors suspecting some sort of wrongdoing by the directors coupled, perhaps, with lack of funds in the liquidation to finance a full investigation by the liquidator.

When a company is wound up by the court, the Official Receiver becomes provisional liquidator. At a later date the Official Receiver may convene a meeting of creditors with a view to appointing an outside liquidator to take over from him and complete the liquidation.

A compulsory liquidation is often viewed as more serious than a creditors' voluntary liquidation: certainly professional advisers would usually counsel the PMD to attempt the creditors' voluntary route rather than wait and face a petition, which, if successful, would then mean a personal examination by the Official Receiver who would thereafter publish his findings.

Since April 1986 however, whichever route is taken, be it receivership, creditors' voluntary liquidation or compulsory liquidation, the receiver or liquidator is *bound by statute to file a report with the Department of Trade, which will include his comments upon the conduct of the directors*, where appropriate. This document will not be available as a matter of public record but will be used as a basis for consolidating information and statistics and may be used by the Department for prosecution purposes.

Which to choose - compulsory liquidation or creditors' voluntary liquidation?

No creditor enjoys hearing that he is likely to incur a bad debt and to him, if his customer has gone into liquidation, it might appear fairly academic whether that liquidation was voluntary or compulsory.

On the other hand, it is not necessarily academic - and to certain individual creditors, it might be anything but academic and could be very important.

We have talked in our question-and-answer section on receivership in the previous section in this chapter about preferences which, if caught in time, are voidable - that is, can be set aside - by a liquidator.

It is the date of liquidation that determines the preference period, so that it is in the interests of any PMD whose company has granted some sort of preference, to attempt to delay any liquidation of his company until after the preference period has expired. It is, conversely, in the interests of creditors generally to get the company into liquidation as quickly as possible.

Suppose a director, knowing his company to be in financial difficulties, repaid an advance of £250,000 to a friend on 1 May. (For purpose of the example, we will assume that this transaction constituted a voidable preference.)

Later that year, on 27 October, a creditor presented a petition for the winding-up of the company, which was due to be heard before the court on 14 December. The directors convened meetings of the members and creditors of the company and placed it into creditors' voluntary liquidation on 30 November.

At the creditors' meeting, mention was made of the petition and the reporting accountant – who was by now the company's nominated liquidator – stated that in his opinion creditors present should agree unanimously that the court be advised they opposed the compulsory winding-up of the company and they wished the petition to lapse.

The nominated liquidator spoke most eloquently; he advised that in his opinion this was a liquidation which needed immediate action and that compulsory liquidation would mean inevitable delays. Moreover, there would be additional fees involved which would make it costlier to creditors than if he simply remained in office as liquidator under the now, in force, (creditors') voluntary liquidation. In any event, the company was already in liquidation, so what was the point of a further unnecessary amendment to the route of the liquidation?

The creditors agreed, for what was said seemed to make sense and they wanted no delays in receiving a possible dividend. The company's nominated liquidator was confirmed by the creditors as the liquidator of the company.

That liquidator had placed his own selfish financial interests before the interests of the creditors and, in so doing, denied them an asset of £250,000.

Impossible, you might say, anyone can work out that the six months preference period had passed by the time the company was placed into liquidation – given that the preferred creditor was not associated with the company, which would have extended the period to two years.

It is true that to catch the preference within six months from 1 May, it would have been necessary for the company to be in liquidation by 1 November and, as it did not go into liquidation until 30 November, the period would seem to have passed.

Not necessarily; whereas the date of liquidation in a creditors' voluntary winding-up is the date that the resolution is passed placing the company into liquidation, the date of liquidation in a compulsory winding-up is, following the making of a winding-up order, *deemed to be the date of presentation of the petition.*

In our example, assuming the winding-up petition presented on 27 October had not been withdrawn and a winding-up order had been made on 14 December, the company's liquidation would have commenced on 27 October, four days before the preference period expired and the liquidator could have demanded repayment of the £250,000.

It was because the company's nominated liquidator was frightened that he might be outvoted at any subsequent creditors' meeting following a compulsory winding-up and because he wanted to ensure he remained as liquidator (and possibly earn a large fee) that he compromised his integrity and deceived the creditors as to the truth of the situation.

Regrettably, events very similar to this have actually occurred, to the shame of those involved.

In chapter 4, we are going to look at the question of the costs involved in liquidating a company and the effect these can have when attempting to determine dividend prospects as disclosed by a statement of affairs.

Summary

The above should form a general guide to the various alternatives available to the PMD whose company faces corporate insolvency. This book can, however, give only general guidance. Any PMD finding his company in financial difficulties should seek expert professional assistance as soon as possible.

One point should always be remembered: since December 1986 all formal insolvency appointments may be taken only by an authorised insolvency practitioner. The Poor Man's solicitor or accountant should be able to advise upon an appropriate choice of nominee.

3 Bankruptcy -
the avoidable option

Background

We have now arrived at the point where our Poor Man has reached the road to bankruptcy.

For some reason personal bankruptcy has throughout the ages been regarded by the English as if it were a criminal – or at least a quasi-criminal – offence. On the other hand a director of a failed company can often escape the stigma that is the fate of the personal debtor and, in some instances, can even attract a sort of notoriety in the form of grudging admiration!

It must, however, be remembered that the Poor Man reading this book must somehow have found himself outside the shield of limited liability and is interested only in his personal fate in its alternative forms.

You may well have been hanged if you did not pay – that is, during the eighteenth century – if you failed to surrender self or entire estate to the Commission of Bankruptcy.

It is hard to believe, as we approach the last decade of the twentieth century, that so Draconian were the penalties for such an offence that upon a complaint by a creditor to the Commission and the charge being upheld, the *only* penalty was death – without the opportunity to commute to transportation. (No chance for the unfortunate descendants to meet the Royal Family in the Australian bicentennial celebrations!)

Take comfort, then, that you are unlikely to share the same fate as Messrs Town, Thompson and Perrott who, being found guilty as charged in 1712, 1756 and 1761 respectively, were all hanged.

The Road to Bankruptcy

Almost anyone can find himself facing bankruptcy; it is no respecter of persons and by no means restricted to those who engage in trade or business.

Take the famous case of the man walking down the street minding his own business when a drayman asked if he would help to lower a barrel of beer into a cellar. The kind-hearted passer-by readily agreed, the barrel slipped, the drayman was injured and the court held the passer-by responsible. It was true that he was under no duty to help, but having agreed to help he was, the court said, then under a duty to exercise all necessary care, even though he was to receive no payment.

The drayman was awarded damages against the otherwise innocent and kind-hearted passer-by. Imagine that case today, the passer-by without the necessary insurance and having virtually no assets – he could well face bankruptcy.

In recent times, we have seen thousands of people – the majority of them elderly – lose their entire life savings following the highly publicised collapse of certain dealers in securities. We will cover the problem of speculative investment and giving of deposits against future contracts, in chapter 4.

However, having said this, it is probable that the Poor Man will have found himself walking the road to bankruptcy via one of two main routes, namely:

1 Through trading without the benefit of limited liability, i.e. as a sole trader or partner in a firm, or
2 As a guarantor of a company bank account.

There are other possibilities, for example as a director of a failed company who has been held personally liable by the court to contribute to the assets of the company following the concept of wrongful trading. The Poor Man finding himself in this situation, however, needs far more than a handy little book and would be best advised to stop reading now and make an immediate appointment with his solicitor.

Whatever the route, the end result is the same – the Poor Man's inability to pay his creditors in full so that he must face bankruptcy or seek some other alternative – but what are the alternatives?

With just the slightest hint of cribbing – and without intending any offence – it is possible to compare the old options before the change (BC) with the new options after December 1986 (AD) and to see how these have improved or impaired the chance of the Poor Man on the road to bankruptcy.

The Option BC

The sad truth was that before the change, the Poor Man on the road to bankruptcy almost inevitably travelled the full journey. It is true that there was an alternative, known as a *Deed of Arrangement*, but this was not popular with the insolvency practitioners because of the inherent difficulties in obtaining the necessary agreement from creditors.

"Behold, Great Impecunious! Their number grows legion"

Neither was it particularly popular with the creditors themselves, who were originally unable to obtain repayment of any VAT element of their claims unless the Poor Man was actually made bankrupt.

The Options AD

After (29th) December, 1986, there is now a second option to formal bankruptcy known as an *Individual Voluntary Arrangement* (as opposed to a *Company Voluntary Arrangement*). The Poor Man could be forgiven for questioning whether the earlier available deed of arrangement was a 'voluntary' arrangement – and it was – but then, clouding the issue has always been a fundamental requirement when drafting new legislation, so we should not be too surprised to find that we now have two 'voluntary' schemes.

Given that the Poor Man now has two possible formal alternatives to straightforward bankruptcy, namely:

1 A Deed of Arrangement (DOA) with his creditors under the Deeds of Arrangement Act 1914; or
2 An Individual Voluntary Arrangement (IVA) with his creditors under the Insolvency Act 1986,

which route is he to choose?

Before we attempt to answer his question, we should remember that the DOA route has been available to the Poor Man and his advisers for over seventy years but because it was not popular with insolvency practitioners the Poor Man, as a consequence, rarely knew that he had at least a chance of escaping bankruptcy and only a handful of DOAs were executed each year.

Let us examine the problems which have made DOAs so unpopular with the professionals, look at the effect that new legislation has had and then we can perhaps consider their future as a viable alternative to either an IVA or bankruptcy.

Deeds of Arrangement

The DOA - BC

The Poor Man had to persuade the majority of his creditors not to make him bankrupt and, as an alternative, to accept a DOA.

An informal meeting of his creditors would usually be called for them to consider his proposals and indicate their feelings. There was nothing to say that creditors should attend, however, and those present could in no way bind those who chose to stay away; if it ever came to a question of formal assent, every creditor, present or not, would be entitled to vote upon acceptance.

If creditors had reason to believe that the debtor had misbehaved – for example by attempting to transfer his assets to relatives – they would be most reluctant to assent to a DOA because a Trustee would not possess the statutory powers to set aside such transactions.

This, then, was (and remains) the fundamental difficulty in avoiding formal bankruptcy, because a Trustee in Bankruptcy, in contrast to a DOA Trustee, had extensive powers to look into and, if appropriate, set aside certain transactions which had taken place anything up to two years before the event. (AD the preference periods are five years for transactions at an undervalue, two years for an associated person and six months for any other preference – see also page 62).

Assuming the creditors could be persuaded to forgo this right of action – presumably on the grounds that they were satisfied nothing untoward had taken place – a new problem arose with the inception of VAT.

When VAT was first introduced, it simply rubbed further salt into the wounds of unsecured creditors, for they themselves had to pay the VAT over to the Customs and Excise, thereby increasing their losses. (This is the start of the 15 per cent penalty discussed on page 46.)

This position was regularised in 1978, when VAT bad debt relief was granted, but it applied only to formal bankruptcies so that creditors were obliged to bankrupt the Poor Man if they were to obtain relief for the VAT they had borne on their debts.

The Poor Man and his advisers who had sufficient motivation remaining to persist along the road of the DOA, countered by appealing to the Poor Man's relatives and friends to raise funds equal to the VAT element of creditors' claims, in an attempt to remove this new factor.

Happily, the anomaly of the situation filtered through to the Government, resulting in an amendment to the legislation in April 1986 which extended VAT bad debt relief to DOAs. (See page 20 for changes following 1990 Budget.)

So far, so good, but we have by no means exhausted all the problems – although by now the problems would have exhausted and did exhaust many a Poor Man (or perhaps his advisers) who might otherwise have been saved.

The next step was to obtain the necessary assents to the Deed – that is, persuade the required number of creditors in value and amount to agree to be bound by it and thereafter attend to its registration.

This aspect of the DOA has never been easy and the time constraints are both difficult and rigidly applied. It is true to say that the formal statutory requirements for satisfactorily executing a DOA have themselves been quite sufficient without other complications to deter many a professional adviser from suggesting this route to his Poor Man client.

Having registered the DOA, the Poor Man was still not in the clear because, BC, the execution of the Deed was itself an 'act of bankruptcy'. In simple terms, this meant that any creditor could turn to the court and plead that the Poor Man should be declared formally bankrupt by virtue of having committed an act of bankruptcy.

These acts of bankruptcy expired after three months, but many professional advisers were reluctant to travel the DOA route because it was difficult, time-consuming and expensive enough to reach the point where the Deed could be registered; to have a creditor then use the existence of the Deed to present a petition for bankruptcy within the following three months was heart-breaking.

The DOA - AD
The new insolvency law has scrapped the concept of Acts of Bank-

ruptcy, so that if the DOA route is followed AD and the Poor Man and his advisers manage to overcome all the hurdles and actually register the Deed, they are now 'home and dry' and the Deed is binding upon any dissenting minority.

This, however, is the only change AD. All other problems remain so that the Poor Man will not be able to ascertain whether or not he has acquired the necessary assents simply by taking a vote at the meeting of creditors – for this is an informal meeting and *all* creditors, present or not, must indicate their acceptance, or otherwise, of the Deed for purpose of arriving at the required majority in favour.

A DOA requires approval by a majority in both number *and* value of all creditors (claims of £10 and under being included for value only).

The Individual Voluntary Arrangement

So much, then, for the DOA, but how does it compare with the newer alternative, the individual voluntary arrangement (IVA)?

It should be realised that the IVA was brought in not simply as an aid to the Poor Man, but to streamline procedures and remove a considerable pressure of work from the country's Official Receivers by placing it into the hands of the authorised insolvency practitioners.

It is likely that the IVA will come to be regarded as a small bankruptcy for, on the Poor Man's own petition, (for formal bankruptcy), the court would not make a bankruptcy order if the total of the unsecured claims were below the 'small bankruptcy level', (at the time of writing, £20,000), the value of his assets not less than the minimum amount, (currently £2,000), and he had neither been bankrupt nor entered into a scheme of arrangement with his creditors within the last five years. The intention would be that the Poor Man would seek an individual voluntary arrangement (IVA).

What is an individual voluntary arrangement?

An IVA is a statutory scheme intended as an alternative to formal bankruptcy now available following legislation contained in the Insolvency Act 1986. It differs from a DOA in that it is authorised by the court whereas a DOA is simply registered with the court. There were early fears that the VAT 15 per cent penalty (see page 46) would, at least initially, apply to IVAs. Happily, this fear has been dispelled by the Customs and Excise and VAT bad debt relief will apply to IVAs just as it applied to DOAs.

IVAs do have practical advantages over DOAs. We have learned that a DOA requires approval by a majority in both number and value of all creditors, excluding, for the purpose of the exercise, all creditors whose claims are £10 or under. In addition, the claims of *all* creditors – whether present or not at the informal meeting to consider the debtors proposals – must be taken into account for purpose of calculating the required majorities.

On the other hand, although an IVA requires acceptance by a majority of 75 per cent of creditors, the required majority

1 is for value only;
2 applies only to the claims of creditors who *actually attend the statutory meeting convened for the purpose of considering the debtor's proposals*, provided proper notice of the meeting was given to all known creditors. (Amounts due to associates of the debtor are excluded for voting purposes.)

Here, then, we see that in the case of an IVA, the creditors' meeting, correctly convened, is a formal meeting following which the Poor Man will know whether or not he has escaped bankruptcy by virtue of having obtained the necessary assents to the IVA.

To highlight the difference between voting procedures in a DOA and an IVA, it is possible in the case of the latter for just one creditor, whose claim amounts to not less than 75 per cent in value of the creditors attending and voting, to bind all creditors to an IVA, whether or not they attend the formal meeting.

Finally, IVAs are easier to get under way than a DOA, and the court has power to make an interim order which has the effect of preventing any creditors taking action against the debtor or his assets during the period of the Order.

Preferences and Transfers at Undervalue

We discussed earlier in this chapter the fundamental difficulty in avoiding bankruptcy where the creditors believed the Poor Man had entered into transactions (which had resulted in a depletion of his estate) that could be challenged only by a Trustee in Bankruptcy.

If any insolvent Poor Man wishes to avoid bankruptcy and hopes to persuade his creditors to approve either a DOA or an IVA as an alternative, then he would do well never

1 to enter into any transaction at an undervalue; nor
2 give any preference within the relevant time, which could (only) be set aside following formal bankruptcy.

The relevant time is within a period before the date of presentation of the bankruptcy petition, and is

a five years in the case of a transaction at undervalue;

b two years in the case of a preference to an associate (other than someone who is purely his employee), and which is not a transaction at an undervalue; and

c six months in any other case of preference which is not a transaction at an undervalue.

So much then for the time-scales, but what sort of preferences are we talking about? Full details are contained in Sections 339 and 340 of the Insolvency Act 1986, and are summarised as follows.

A transaction is deemed to be at undervalue if:

1 it is gifted or the terms of the transaction result in no consideration being received; or

2 it is entered into with a person in consideration of marriage; or

3 the consideration for the transaction is significantly less in money's worth than the value of the asset which has been transferred.

A transaction is deemed to constitute a preference to a person if:

a that person is a creditor of the individual or a surety or guarantor for any of his debts and liabilities; and

b the individual does something or allows something to be done which effectively places that person in a better position than he otherwise would have been in the event of the individual's bankruptcy.

Summary

In the majority of instances, there should be no need for the Poor Man simply to give up and allow himself to be made bankrupt. He now has not one, but two alternatives, namely a DOA or an IVA.

Which one to choose?

It is inevitable that we will see far more IVAs in the future than we will DOAs.

Nevertheless, the DOA route holds certain attractions, not least of which is its general informality, including the avoidance of any court procedure (except to the extent that the information is placed on the court file). To some, at least, it is a further step removed from bankruptcy than is an IVA and there will always be the Poor Man client who would hope to persuade his financial adviser to seek the DOA route.

The purpose of this section of the book, however, is not to suggest either route as being preferable to the other, for much will depend upon the individual circumstances. Rather it is an attempt to let the Poor Man know that he does have two viable alternatives to bankruptcy, so that, given his difficulties, he would, armed with this book, go and see his accountant or solicitor to discuss the problems and the way forward – rather than walking round to the Official Receiver's office or allowing a creditor to petition for his bankruptcy.

The way forward!

If it saves just one Poor Man from Bankruptcy, it will have achieved that purpose.

The execution of Perrott in 1761 (see page 55).

4 Common Considerations

Personal Guarantees

In this chapter we are going to look in greater detail at personal guarantees, given in support of a company's borrowings.

Occasionally a supplier might agree not to press a claim for an unpaid account, or agree to give further extended credit terms, if the PMD were to sign a personal guarantee undertaking to settle any outstanding amount out of his own resources in the event of the company's insolvency. There is little that can be said which is not already obvious. 'Don't do it,' would be the immediate initial response. The financial situation of the company must already be questionable if this position has been reached.

It is, of course, possible that a major supplier required that a personal guarantee be incorporated into his trading terms at a time when the company first commenced to trade and the PMD simply viewed the situation as part of the company's financial structure.

As a working rule, every PMD should refuse to sign a personal guarantee in support of trade supplies unless and until he has discussed the matter with his solicitor and either accepted his judgment or braced himself for the possible consequences of his intended action.

The position is somewhat different where banks are concerned and it may be that there is no alternative to the PMD giving his personal guarantee and taking on a potential, personal liability, if the required funding is to be forthcoming.

Any guarantee is only as good as the guarantor's ability to meet this liability and the guarantee of a director who is 'not worth powder and shot', is useless.

Banks like to see their security in the form of tangible assets and if they rely upon personal guarantees as part of that security, will often require the guarantee be itself supported by a charge over a tangible asset – which usually turns out to be the director's house. This obviates any problems over ability to repay.

What is does not obviate is the distressing necessity to place the guarantor and his family amongst the ranks of the homeless if the security needs to be realised. (If it needs to be said, any Poor Man husband should have a very serious and soul-searching discussion with his spouse before pledging the family home in support of a business guarantee.)

It is because the banks are reluctant to force any guarantor to sell his home that, where possible, they would prefer their collateral charge to be over a non-domestic property. This is possible more frequently than might be suspected.

The explanation is quite simple. Many a PMD will have been advised by his financial adviser that, for reasons of tax efficiency in his

67

particular circumstances, it would be more advantageous if he, rather than the company, owned title to the trading premises. In such instances, any charge given will cover property owned by the PMD personally and, as such, becomes collateral security, securing the company's borrowings.

It is here there lies latent a seldom considered but potentially disastrous pitfall to which earlier indication was given in chapter 1.

The effect of the pitfall is to create a 'taxation trap' which undoes and indeed reverses all the intended tax-saving benefits which were to be achieved through personal ownership of the property.

The problem can best be demonstrated by way of a simple example. Our PMD purchases property in his own name for £30,000 and gives a charge over this to the bank as security for an overdraft facility of like amount being made available to his company. Five years later, after a period that saw rapid escalation in property values during which time the rate of inflation was relatively low, the property has a market value of £200,000. The company's trade has also dramatically increased and the bank has generously allowed its overdraft facility to rise in line with the value of the security.

Then comes the crunch: world fashion changes, the company's product becomes obsolete, the company has to stop trading and the bank requires the property to be sold, taking the entire proceeds to pay off the company's overdraft.

So, where is the problem – hasn't the bank been paid in full and the guarantee satisfied? Indeed it has, but what everyone forgot when the guarantee was given, was that silent, invisible partner, who waits patiently to claim his lawful entitlement to a share of any eventual profits – the taxman.

It is always possible that future legislation might remove the taxation on capital gains which has been with us (with varying degrees of relief) since 1965, but until such time, provision is necessary.

In our present example, the property has increased in value by £170,000 and, even after allowing some adjustment for inflation (referred to technically as indexation), it would not be unrealistic to expect a tax assessment on the capital gain of at least £50,000 – and it could be over £60,000.

The bank will not pay the tax; its charge entitles it to the entire proceeds of sale and the taxman will turn to the individual who has (if only theoretically) enjoyed the benefit of the gain. It is not, after all, the taxman's fault that the PMD had pledged his putative profits elsewhere.

So, what *should* the PMD do when it comes to giving the bank a charge on personal property to secure his company's borrowings?

At the moment, we see him hopping unhappily from one prong of the fork to the other. On the one hand, if he gives a charge over his home, any increase in value should (normally) be tax free, but he faces having to sell the house to pay the guarantee.

On the other hand, if he grants a charge on property other than his personal private residence he faces the tax pitfall described above, which might result in his having to sell his home after all to pay the tax arising and, in extreme circumstances, face personal bankruptcy.

It is obviously preferable, wherever possible, not to grant charges over private residences. Having said this, there is often no other viable alternative and the PMD needs to weigh carefully the potential profits and benefits against the consequences of failure and decide whether the exercise is worth the risk: whether it is a good idea after all to 'speculate to accumulate'.

Where the PMD does own other property, there are two very positive steps that he can take; one of them he most definitely *should* take. Which one, will depend upon the particular circumstances.

He should first of all remind the bank of the invisible partner who is entitled by statute to a calculated share of any increase in value of the property and require that a clause be inserted into the bank's charge restricting it to the net proceeds of any eventual sale *after* providing for payment of any capital gains tax arising from the sale.

The bank may not accept such a restriction, particularly where the property has already been held for some time and its current value is needed in full to cover the required facility. Should this prove to be the case he will need to consider the alternative. It might be possible, with proper advice, to address the capital gains tax problem sooner rather than later by 'selling' or gifting the property to the company. This would be particularly appropriate where we are dealing with office, factory or warehouse property occupied by the company as tenant. *If this is contemplated great care will be needed to avoid creating immediate taxation problems, and specialist advice is essential.*

Whatever happens, the PMD should never place himself in the position of being personally exposed to having to find capital gains tax arising on the enforced sale of a personal asset, where the entire proceeds of sale have been taken in payment of a guarantee given to support company borrowings.

There is another instance when a guarantor could find that what he thought was to be a simple, unsupported guarantee was actually secured through a prior charge on his house. This could occur when his house mortgage was already with the same bank to whom he subsequently gives a simple guarantee – even though the two transactions were otherwise totally unconnected.

This position is unlikely to occur very often because the bank manager should explain the consequences of the earlier security extending to future borrowings at the time the guarantee is discussed.

There could be instances, however, when, with the best will in the world, the bank manager fails to detect or advise against a potential pitfall, with financially disastrous consequences; this is when we come to *joint and several guarantees.*

It is first of all necessary to understand the terminology. A joint and several guarantee is one which is entered into by two or more parties in support of the same liability, and where each party is individually liable for the full amount of the guarantee.

Suppose a bank offers an overdraft facility of £90,000 to a company if its three directors will agree to enter into a joint and several guarantee for £90,000 plus interest.

This would not mean that the bank could collect 3×£90,000, that is £270,000, if it called in the guarantees. What it does mean is that the bank can, at its option, call upon any or all of the directors to meet their guarantees up to the full amount of £90,000 plus accrued interest. What it does *not* mean is that each guarantor will be called upon individually to pay £30,000 plus interest.

The first problem with this type of guarantee is that the personal circumstances of the guarantors may have changed dramatically between the giving of the guarantee and the call from the bank demanding payment under the terms of the guarantee. It may well be that all these guarantors had similar financial strength when they started out but, for whatever reason – perhaps divorce or unfortunate investment – if only one of them has any money at the time the guarantee is called upon, the banks are perfectly entitled to look to that individual for payment of the whole sum.

There is a second problem with joint and several guarantees. Suppose the bank demands the entire proceeds from one of the three guarantors. It might be thought this Poor Man guarantor could bring his co-guarantors into the action so as somehow to limit his contribution to £30,000. Unhappily, this is not the case; he would have to pay the full amount and, only when he had paid, would he then be able to commence action against the two other guarantors for a 'right of contribution'.

Wherever possible, it is obviously preferable to attempt to negotiate with the bank from the outset and agree that three separate individual guarantees of £30,000 be taken as an alternative to the requested joint and several guarantees.

The bank may not agree, in which case any would-be guarantor must address his mind to what might result should the worst happen. He should also ask himself why the bank refuses to agree and apply the acid test first discussed in chapter 1.

If things are so good, why are things so bad?

Why won't the bank split the liability; is the risk greater than originally anticipated and are his co-guarantors men of straw?

It is when we come to joint and several guarantees supported by a charge over property – and particularly where any one guarantor has a greater equity in that property than the others – that we come across the potential pitfall, which even the bank manager might fail to spot and point out at the time the guarantee and security are given.

Rather than try to explain the pitfall in theoretical terms, we can best understand the problem by reference to a real-life example. The story is told in full in chapter 5.

No would-be joint and several guarantor should ever contemplate offering fixed charges on property in support of that guarantee without learning from the experience of Poor Man Partner A.

Meetings of Creditors

There are a number of occasions when a company may convene a meeting of its creditors to discuss and perhaps vote upon proposals that could affect their chances of receiving payment.

These would include meetings convened:

- by the company to consider a creditors' voluntary liquidation.
- by the Official Receiver following the making of a winding-up or bankruptcy order, to consider the appointment of a liquidator or trustee.
- by an administrator of a company to consider his proposals.
- by the nominee of a company or an individual to consider a voluntary arrangement.
- by an administrative receiver to consider his report and to appoint a committee of creditors.

Creditors will usually be concerned with the first type of meeting (known formally as a meeting convened under Section 98 of the Insolvency Act 1986) to consider a creditors' voluntary liquidation, and it is upon such meetings that we concentrate our attention.

Whether a creditor decides to attend a creditors' meeting will usually depend upon the circumstances surrounding his claim. If he feels particularly aggrieved at the way he believes he has been treated, he will be more inclined to attend and remonstrate with the directors than if he simply writes his unsecured claim off as bad luck. He does, however, have the opportunity of sending his representative to attend in his stead and vote upon any resolution.

The statutory purpose of convening formal meetings of creditors is to allow the unsecured creditors the opportunity to vote upon one or more resolution. In order to be able to vote, the creditor has to be present personally or by proxy. Forms of proxy should be sent out to all creditors along with the notice convening the meeting. The only creditor who can be present personally and vote without having submitted a valid proxy is a sole trader to whom the debt is personally due.

In any other case, the person attending, be it a partner in a firm or a director of a limited company, must be named on a valid proxy that has been lodged specifically for the purpose of voting on the specific resolution.

It may seem strange that a director is allowed to complete a form of proxy, naming himself for voting purposes when he is not allowed to vote unless he has dealt with this legal formality, and perhaps even stranger that a partner in a firm must go through the same procedure, but the law upon the subject is quite clear.

Forms of proxy tend to be much simpler and easier to complete than they were in times past, although care still needs to be taken to ensure that there are no mistakes which would cause them to be invalidated on some technical ground.

It has not been unknown – particularly before liquidators had to be authorised insolvency practitioners – for unscrupulous directors to attempt to procure the appointment of a 'cowboy' liquidator of their choice in either the belief or knowledge that he would thereafter run the liquidation for the benefit of everyone except the creditors. It is easy to understand why such people would use any excuse to declare potentially hostile proxy holders unable to vote against their own chosen appointee!

Suppose it is important to you that you be allowed to vote for a liquidator of your own choice. You should make certain that your proxy is correctly completed; follow the instructions on, or given with, the form and, if you are in any doubt, seek the assistance of an expert.

A word of warning to creditors who have reason to believe that special circumstances surround their claims and suspect they may be secured. There is nothing to stop a secured creditor from attending the meeting of creditors and observing the conduct of the meeting. A secured creditor may not, however, vote upon a resolution to appoint a liquidator *unless he surrenders his security to the value of his vote.*

Security may not necessarily mean having taken and registered charges on the company's assets. There are times when a company is deemed to hold specific funds for specific creditors *in trust.* Again, many reservation-of-title clauses stipulate that any monies received in payment for goods which have been supplied, must be held in a special bank account until such time as remitted to them. Although we usually find that this requirement is ignored, it is possible that a liquidator might discover a *constructive trust.* In these circumstances, the specific creditor's claims may have been secured upon these monies and for this creditor to have submitted a proxy and voted upon it at a creditors' meeting may well disenfranchise him from that security.

The motto is quite simple; if you believe that there are special circumstances surrounding your claim and that you are not necessarily and automatically an *unsecured* creditor, you should take expert legal opinion at the earliest opportunity and until such time do not sign any further documentation in connection with or in support of your claim.

When completing the form of proxy, always try to arrange for at least one other person to be able to attend as an alternative to your initial choice of proxy holder and make sure that both are named on the proxy as alternative holders. You can never be certain; if you name yourself as first-named you could be ill and unable to go. There again, if you named someone else he may win the pools before the date fixed for the meeting and lose all interest in your financial problems!

You will need to intimate your claim in the liquidation before it comes to the time to vote. The safest way to do this is to include copies of any outstanding invoices, together with a statement and enclose these when returning the completed proxy.

If the meeting is convened by the Official Receiver, for example in a bankruptcy or compulsory liquidation, you will be required to complete a Proof of Debt, which asks for even more information.

The proxy must be returned to the address named in the notice for the purpose and, by the time specified, which will be a given hour, usually on the day preceding the meeting.

The form of proxy will normally be a combined form which allows it to be completed as a *general* or a *special* proxy. Complete it as a general proxy if you want the proxy holder to vote upon a resolution after having heard all that is to be said upon the subject and you wish to reserve judgment until then. Complete it as a special proxy if you wish to instruct the proxy holder to vote in a specific manner, having already decided in advance the course you wish to follow.

There is provision for the chairman of the meeting to be named as either your general or special proxy. If you appoint the chairman as your special proxy holder, he must vote on the resolution in accordance with your written instructions contained in the proxy.

If, however, you simply name the chairman as your general proxy, he will use your vote as he thinks fit – which, in practice, usually means he will vote in the manner which pleases him (and may not please the other creditors present). Remember that the chairman of a meeting convened for the purpose of appointing a liquidator will be a director of the failed company, and he is likely to use his general proxies to support his own choice of liquidator.

If being able to vote is important, the completed documentation should be taken round by hand, or sent by special delivery, and a receipt obtained confirming the time and date of delivery.

If, in an effort to recover your debt, you have already instructed a trade protection association or a firm of solicitors to act for you some time previously, you may find that all the paperwork, including the proxy form, has been forwarded to your agents.

One service which all trade protection associations offer, free of charge, is to have a representative attend any meeting of creditors on behalf of their Poor Man unsecured creditor member and obtain a written report upon what transpired. This free service is also offered by most accountancy firms which have specialist insolvency or corporate recovery departments. In many cases, the trade associations utilise the services of authorised insolvency practitioners and rely upon them for attendance and reporting purposes.

An understanding of how the system works will help to explain why any professional person is prepared to attend a meeting at his own expense and issue a comprehensive report thereon, free of charge.

The liquidator will be appointed by those creditors present and able to vote at the meeting convened for the purpose, and his appointment will be secured by a simple majority in value of those voting.

We will come to the question of liquidators' fees in a little while but for the purpose of the illustration let us accept that most liquidators will receive a fee for their services and that generally the larger the value of the assets involved in any case, the larger the liquidator's eventual remuneration. It is, therefore, quite normal to notice that the interest of authorised insolvency practitioners, from whose ranks the liquidator must be appointed, increases in direct proportion to the size of the assets involved.

Many authorised practitioners are skilled speakers; a handful are experienced advocates and it is often through a blend of these skills, combined with a flair for rhetoric, that the votes of creditors present might well be influenced. Thus, it is important for those who specialise in insolvency and rely upon appointments for their own or their firm's livelihood to attend these meetings, and every proxy which is lodged in their direct or indirect favour affords an opportunity of procuring an appointment.

It is not unknown, following a meeting of creditors, for ordinary trade creditors to be heard to criticise the professional element present on the grounds that they had been scoring points off one another, in a manner that had nothing to do with protecting the interests of their clients. This has certainly been known to happen on the odd occasion but, by and large, the criticism is unjustified. It was Shakespeare who wrote,

> All the world's a stage and all the men and women merely players . . .,

and it must be conceded that a creditors' meeting provides an excellent forum for some specialists to demonstrate their thespian skills. It is this art of delivery, a skill in its own right, which can persuade creditors present to support the viewpoint and objective of the speaker.

The purpose of a statutory meeting of creditors convened under Section 98 of the Insolvency Act 1986 is to appoint a liquidator and there have been occasions when the chairman of a meeting has attempted to restrict the business of the meeting to that single purpose. It is, however, usual – as already described in chapter 2 – for a report upon the company's history and its current financial position to be given to the meeting as a courtesy to creditors, and for creditors to be invited to ask questions of the directors and the reporting accountant.

It is often only as a result of skilful questioning from the floor of the meeting by a professional present, that vital information is gleaned which would otherwise never have become known to the creditors.

It is because of this that no trade creditor should deny availing himself of the opportunity to enjoy the one free service he is likely to obtain either from, or through, his accountant, and take along an expert with him to the meeting of creditors rather than attempt to 'fire his own bullets'.

At a typical meeting of creditors, convened for the purpose of appointing a liquidator, the agenda would be as follows:

1 Introduction of 'top table' by reporting accountant.
2 Report to meeting upon the company's trading history and events that have led to the financial collapse.
3 Statement of affairs read out with pertinent explanations.
4 Meeting open to questions.
5 Vote taken upon appointment of liquidator.
6 Election of a liquidation committee.

The liquidation committee, which usually comprises three or five creditors elected to represent all creditors, acts to guide the liquidator upon certain aspects of the liquidation. For example, it could approve the discontinuance of legal actions where, in the committee's opinion, the risk and costs involved outweigh the prospects of further recoveries. Quite often a committee will insist that the liquidator follow up a matter which he has either overlooked or neglected.

Another function of the committee is to approve the liquidator's remuneration (a topic we will cover in the next chapter).

In short, the committee acts to both assist in, and at the same time monitor, the course and conduct of the liquidation.

Under normal circumstances, membership is not an onerous burden and it is possible to have 'telephone meetings' to dispose of minor points. It should, however, be realised that although the liquidator can defray the expenses of the committee incurred in attending a meeting of creditors, he is not empowered to compensate them for their actual time involved.

For most creditors, the real purpose in attending a meeting of creditors is to find out what has happened and to assess their prospects of any eventual dividend upon their claims. This assessment will be made in the light of the statement of affairs, supplemented by any further information, given or extracted at the meeting.

In the next section we are going to discuss the reading and interpretation of a statement of affairs. It is this document, which must be laid before the meeting, that gives an indication to the various class of creditor and any guarantors as to what a particular liquidation could mean to them in financial terms.

Statements of Affairs

We have from time to time throughout the text talked in general terms about a statement of affairs. Now we are going to consider a statement of affairs in more detail. Everyone who has been in business will be familiar with a balance sheet. Every company is obliged to prepare a balance sheet drawn up to the date of its year end and even small businesses will normally require a balance sheet to satisfy their local Inspector of Taxes before agreeing their taxation assessment.

The balance sheet sets out in analysed detail the capital that is employed in the company, i.e. capital introduced plus profits subsequently earned (or less losses subsequently sustained) and the manner in which that capital, augmented by loans from banks and credit given from suppliers, is utilised. (On pages 17 and 18 we detailed the assets that we could typically expect to find in a company when we considered the separate question of categorising those assets under fixed and floating charges.)

So, if we are content to rely upon balance sheets to give us some indication as to the value of a business when assessing its worth as a going concern, why do we need to start talking about a different document and how does this new document – the statement of affairs – differ from a balance sheet which could have been produced as at the same date?

It is simply because we are having to consider the company in the context of an insolvent situation that the drawing up of a balance sheet in its usual form is not appropriate. A balance sheet is constructed in a manner that groups liabilities by reference to a time factor, e.g. current- or medium-term. It does *not* group them into their various classes such as *secured* or *preferential* and neither does it necessarily identify any specific assets that might be charged to cover certain liabilities. A statement of affairs is, in effect, drawn up to answer a different set of questions – questions which cannot be answered by looking at a balance sheet.

The simplified flow chart overleaf shows how a typical statement of affairs might be compiled.

It should be apparent from the chart that a statement of affairs builds up to show how each individual class of creditor is likely to fare in the liquidation, with any surplus from a higher class, in terms of security, being passed on to form a fund available for the next rank of creditors. The various classes of creditor, in order of priority, are:

1 Secured by fixed charges (see page 17)
2 Preferential creditors (see page 19)
3 Secured by floating charges (see page 18)
4 Unsecured

We can demonstrate how this priority effect operates by looking at a worked example of a statement of affairs prepared for a creditors' meeting convened (under Section 98 of the Insolvency Act 1986) to appoint a liquidator. Such an example is set out on page 81.

Fig. 4.1 The compilation of a typical Statement of Affairs

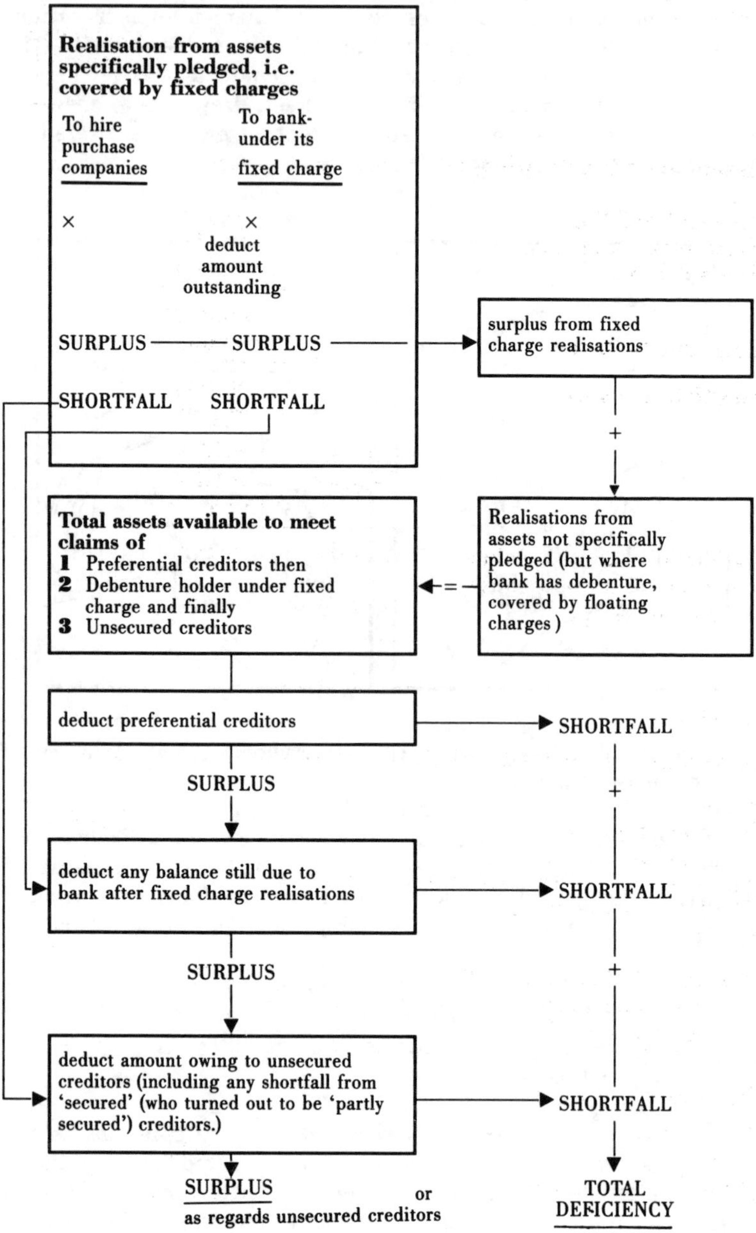

Table 4.1 *Estimated Statement of Affairs of Financial Problems Ltd as at 31 February 1989*

		Estimated realisable values
	£	£
Assets specifically pledged (Fixed-charge assets)		
Freehold buildings	40,000	
Fixed plant & machinery	18,000	
Trade debtors	42,000	
	100,000	
Less: due to bank	130,000	
Shortfall to contra	30,000	

	Motor Vehicles	Machines on Hire Purchase
Estimated realisable values	10,000	20,000
Less: due to hire-purchase companies	12,000	16,000
	2,000	

Surplus	4,000
Assets not specifically pledged (Floating-charge assets)	
Stock	8,000
Work in progress	28,000
Fixtures and fittings	6,000
Motor vehicles (not on hire purchase)	7,000
Plant & machinery (non-fixed)	4,000
ESTIMATED TOTAL ASSETS available for preferential creditors, debenture holder covered by a floating charge and unsecured creditors, subject to the costs of Receivership	57,000

Preferential creditors

VAT	9,000	
PAYE & NIC	11,000	
Bank for wages paid	12,000	32,000
		25,000

continued overleaf

81

Table 4.1 Continued

Due to debenture holder under a floating charge (£30,000–£12,000)		18,000
ESTIMATED SURPLUS as regards debenture holder		7,000
Unsecured creditors		
Trade & expense	60,000	
PAYE, NIC & VAT (non-preferential)	14,000	
Redundancy payments	13,000	
Shortfall to hire-purchase company per contra	2,000	89,000
ESTIMATED DEFICIENCY as regards unsecured creditors		(82,000)
'Share capital' – ordinary shares of £1 each		1,000
ESTIMATED TOTAL DEFICIENCY		(83,000)

The very first thing we notice is that the statement of affairs (the professionals will often be heard referring to this document as 'the S/A') is estimated. Well, of course, it has to be, since no one can predict the exact amounts that individual assets might realise until offers have been made and payment received. It is important, however, that all estimates are predicted as accurately as possible. Thus, where freehold/leasehold property or chattel assets are concerned, it is usual to have these valued by independent experts and those values (as opposed to actual costs or their written-down book values) included as 'estimated realisable values'.

Book debts will always come in for special scrutiny and due provision made to cover any potential bad debts. Certain types of insolvency will always attract the need for a larger than usual write-down in book debts. One obvious example is the contracting industry, where monies due on contracts not yet completed are likely to be offset against claims arising for breach of contract and retention monies to disappear against a sudden plethora of claims for remedial work.

Stocks are liable to claims for reservation of title (see pages 4–5) and may need to be adjusted to take account of valid claims, although in practice the directors should most prudently refuse to accept any reservation of title claims, simply indicating to creditors that certain claims have been received, leaving it to a liquidator to deal with their validity.

Although most of the items appearing on the S/A will either have been already covered in earlier chapters of the book, or alternatively be self-explanatory, there are one or two which are not so obvious and which require some explanation.

The first is the figure of £12,000 shown as 'bank for wages paid' under the heading of preferential creditors. We have already noted that banks prefer to see their security in the form of fixed charges, but that where this is not possible *their floating charges are effective only after the claims of the preferential creditors have been satisfied.*

It is because of this that the banks are quick to take advantage of the old saying 'If you can't beat 'em, join 'em!'

Included in the list of preferential creditors (see page 19) are 'Employees for arrears of holiday pay and (with a current maximum of £800 per employee) up to four months' arrears of wages'. Where, however, the bank has paid the employees' wages and holiday pay, the preferential claim which the employees would have had (had they not been paid) is subrogated to the bank (which has paid them), which is then able effectively to 'stand in the shoes of the employees' and ranks in the insolvency as a preferential creditor to the extent of those advances.

The calcuation of the bank's claim can be quite complicated and its rights can be eroded or even wiped out as a result of monies being paid into the credit of the current account in the ordinary course of

business. (This follows a court decision referred to by the insolvency specialists as Clayton's Case.)

To counteract the decision in Clayton's Case, banks frequently require that the overdraft facility offered to the company is split to create what they call a 'wages account'. Arithmetically, this makes no difference whatsoever to the PMD; indeed, if he is a guarantor to the overdraft it could help by virtue of preserving the bank's preferential claim in any insolvency. *What it must inevitably mean, however, is that the bank is concerned as to its security and should always place the PMD on notice that a receivership could be in the wind.*

In our example, the fact that the bank can establish a preferential wages claim is only of technical interest; it is, in any event, going to recover its monies in full. (Subject, of course, to the estimated asset values being realised and – equally important – to the costs of realisation.)

Where it can make a significant difference to a PMD guarantor is if the bank's fixed charges are insufficient to cover its indebtedness and there is going to be a shortfall to the preferential creditors.

This situation must mean that there can be no surplus from floating charge realisations to pay to the bank after paying the preferential creditors all the proceeds of realisation. However, any dividend that the bank can obtain on a preferential wages claim will mean that much less for the PMD guarantor to find from his own pocket when it comes to meeting his guarantee for the shortfall.

The following example should demonstrate the point.

Assume that the bank is owed £350,000, that is recovers £200,000 under its fixed charges, and that there are floating charge assets with a value of £70,400 and third-party preferential claims totalling £80,000.

The calculation of the guarantor's liability to the bank will be:

	£	£
Total bank borrowings	350,000	
Less recovered under fixed charges	200,000	
Shortfall to bank		**150,000**
Floating charge assets	70,400	
Less owing to preferential creditors	80,000	
Shortfall to preferential creditors	(9,600)	
Surplus available for bank		nil
Guarantor's liability		**150,000**

Suppose, however, that it was possible to establish that the bank had a preferential wages claim in the sum of £80,000.

The calculation now, would be:

	£	£
Total bank borrowings	350,000	
Less recovered under fixed charges	200,000	
Shortfall to bank		**150,000**
Floating charge assets	70,400	
Less owing to preferential creditors:		
Bank 80,000		
Others 80,000	160,000	
Shortfall to preferential creditors	(89,600)	
Dividend available to preferential creditors equals £70,400 ÷ £160,000 = 44 pence in £1		
The bank will therefore receive a dividend of £80,000×0.44, i.e.		35,200
Guarantor's liability		**114,800**

The guarantor's position has improved by £35,200 by virtue of lifting £80,000 of its otherwise unsecured advances to the status of preferential creditor.

Of course such a move, however lawful, does not necessarily achieve any better dividend. There was, many years ago, a famous Leeds insolvency practitioner, long since gone to his eternal reward, who addressed a meeting of creditors at some length, only to conclude by advising the meeting that there would be no dividend for anyone. At the end of his address, a voice was heard from the back of the room enquiring whether he had heard properly and was it true that no one was to receive anything. The liquidator so confirmed. 'But how can this be?', cried the creditor, 'do you realise that I'm preferential?' 'That's right,' said the liquidator, his face an impassive mask, 'we told you first.'

The second situation in the statement of affairs which requires explanation is the inclusion of redundancy payments under the heading of unsecured creditors.

Since the concept of redundancy payments was introduced, the cost to the employer has progressively increased. The idea was that the employer paid the redundancy monies in full and then claimed a percentage rebate from the government. It is this rebate that has been gradually reduced over the years and now stands at 35 per cent of the total redundancy payments. However, *where an employer has ten or more employees he now receives no rebate whatsoever.*

Once the company becomes formally insolvent, the Redundancy Payments Office (RPO – its own abbreviation) of the Department of Employment will fund the entire cost of the redundancy payments and then rank *unsecured* in the insolvency for the payments made, less any rebate which would have been due.

What is not always appreciated is that the RPO will consider funding redundancy payments where a company is attempting to reconstruct to avoid a formal insolvency, but is without the cash resources to fund the payments. Any arrangement will require repayment of the employer's share of the advance as soon as financial circumstances allow.

Whilst on the subject of redundancy payments, it might be appropriate to consider generally the rights of employees following the insolvency of their employer.

The Employment Protection (Consolidation) Act 1978 (as amended) defines the various states of insolvency and contains provisions which will normally allow, within stated limits, for the Department of Employment to settle employees' unpaid remuneration: arrears of pay, holiday pay and pay in lieu of notice. The Department then, in turn, claims in the insolvency; claims for arrears of pay and holiday pay are preferential, a claim for pay in lieu of notice being unsecured.

It is up to the individual employees to make their own claims for any redundancy settlement, although, in practice, a liquidator, AR or administrator should be able to help by putting them in touch with the local RPO.

The position is different when it comes to claims for arrears of pay, holiday pay or pay in lieu of notice. The liquidator, AR or administrator is required to assist in processing these claims and is actually paid a separate fee by the Department of Employment for this work.

The Department of Employment publishes a series of very useful booklets on employment legislation which are regularly updated. Their current booklets Numbers 2 and 3, being *Redundancy Consultation and Notification* and *Employee's Rights on Insolvency of Employer* respectively, contain a great deal of helpful information.

It is the receiver's, administrator's or liquidator's duty to hand to each employee, upon dismissal, a copy of this latter booklet. Until he confirms to the Department of Employment that this has been done, the Department will refuse to start to process any claims in the insolvency.

There are two other entries forming part of the statement of affairs which require obvious explanation. The first, simply explained, is the entry of £14,000 for State debts under the heading of unsecured creditors.

Although VAT, PAYE and NIC are normally preferential claims, they are subject to time (as opposed to monetary) limits and if they have been outstanding for periods in excess of those limits any further amounts outstanding, namely VAT for more than 6 months, PAYE and NIC for more than 12 months, rank as unsecured claims.

The second item is the figure of £1,000 for share capital. When a company is insolvent it is not only the creditors who lose their money. The first losers are the shareholders as regards their share capital and we need to bring their loss into account in order to arrive at the total estimated deficiency.

There remains one hidden assumption in the statement of affairs which requires clarification (although we were given a preview on page 32). We see that whereas a surplus in the value of machinery on hire-purchase arises over the total of the instalments outstanding, a short-fall shown as ranking unsecured is anticipated in respect of the motor vehicles on hire purchase.

In reality, there is every chance that the same hire-purchase company will be involved and, if so, that it will operate a consolidation clause in all its agreements. In other words, it will take £2,000 of the anticipated surplus under one agreement to offset its anticipated loss on the other.

The amounts here are relatively small, but the principle is very important. The hire-purchase company may well have much greater security than is afforded under a single agreement, particularly if there is a lot of equity in an earlier agreement where much of the borrowing has been paid.

Given that interest rates are calculated to reflect the level of risk to the lender, then where large amounts are involved and an earlier agreement would disclose a substantial surplus upon an immediate determination, there is every good reason to require the hire-purchase company to give credit for this extra security when setting the interest rate in a new, parallel (consolidation clause) hire-purchase agreement.

It is in the interests of every individual PMD who guarantees a series of hire-purchase agreements entered into by his company to seek consolidation. If he does not, he could find that in an insolvency he is liable for any shortfalls on individual agreements, with any surplus on the others being paid over to an AR, administrator or liquidator.

One final point, before we attempt to analyse and draw conclusions from the S/A itself, concerns the VAT element of the unsecured creditors' claims. Until the company is actually in liquidation, it is not possible for unsecured creditors to reclaim the VAT bad debt relief which is, in effect, a repayment to them by HM Customs and Excise of the VAT output tax which they have suffered in addition to their specific trading loss. (But see also page 20 for changes following 1990 Budget.)

The actual paperwork is dealt with by the liquidator, following liquidation. It is usual, therefore, to see the claims of unsecured creditors quoted gross, inclusive of any VAT element and, it is hoped, individual claims will reduce by their VAT element following liquidation.

In reality, there is little point in trying to work out whether unsecured creditors' dividend prospects are likely to improve on this count; inevitably, there will be late claims, or previously unknown claims, which will come to light after the date of liquidation and more than compensate for the 15 per cent or so reduction.

We are now almost ready to work out the dividend prospects of each class of creditor, but we are unable to do so until we adjust for one figure which is always omitted from any statement of affairs – the anticipated fees and costs of the liquidator (AR, administrator or trustee) and his agents.

An AR will almost always charge his fees on the basis of time involved. These have to be approved by the debenture holder and, if necessary, justified in due course to the company or an eventual liquidator.

In liquidations and bankruptcies it is usual to charge a fee based upon a percentage of the sum of the assets realised and dividends paid

to creditors, although in the former case, and particularly where substantial figures are involved, a time-cost basis is becoming increasingly
common.

In bankruptcies the trustee's remuneration may be fixed by either
the creditors or the court. In a liquidation, it is usually agreed by a
liquidation committee made up of unsecured creditors. In any dis-
agreement it is always open to a liquidator to seek the court's
guidance.

It is impossible to generalise as to the likely cost involved in any
specific case. One guideline that can be used as a yardstick for calculating a liquidator's or trustee's remuneration is the scale of charges
operated by the Official Receiver when he acts in his capacity of liquidator or trustee. This is the very minimum that is likely to be charged.
The Official Receiver's hourly rate is effectively subsidised by virtue of
other fees charged by the Department of Trade that are not available
to authorised insolvency practitioners.

The scale, which is subject to infrequent review, is currently:

> 20 per cent of the first £5,000 realised
> 15 per cent of the next £5,000 realised
> 10 per cent of the next £90,000 realised, and
> 5 per cent on all subsequent realisations

In addition, an amount equal to half this scale is charged on distri-
butions made to unsecured creditors.

In a typical receivership, the costs to be deducted from realisations will comprise the fees and disbursements of:

1 The administrative receiver
2 His agents for sale of the assets; and
3 His solicitors for conveyancing, debt collection, general legal advice, etc.

If, subsequently, the company proceeds to liquidation, there will be the additional costs of the liquidator and the statutory *ad valorem* fees (i.e. based upon the amounts involved) charged by the Department of Trade.

All in all, insolvency can be an expensive business and the overall costs in percentage terms can be very high indeed.

It might be helpful to attempt to see what sort of effect the application of likely minimum fees might have upon our S/A (pages 81–82).

As it stands,

1 The bank, which is owed £130,000, will recover £100,000 under its fixed charges, £12,000 under its preferential claim, and the balance of £18,000 under its floating charge, leaving a surplus for unsecured creditors of £7,000.
2 One hire-purchase creditor will be paid in full and the other suffer a shortfall of £2,000.
3 The preferential creditors will be paid in full; and
4 There will be £7,000 available, for unsecured creditors owed a total of £89,000, which would enable them to receive a dividend of 7.87 pence in the £1 on their claims.

If we now incorporate estimated likely fees and costs into our statement of affairs, it could appear as follows:

	Estimated to realise	Agents fees	Legal costs	Net proceeds
	£	£	£	£
Assets specifically pledged				
Freehold buildings	40,000	1,000	1,000	38,000
Fixed plant & machinery	18,000	2,000	—	16,000
Trade debtors	42,000	—	2,000	40,000
				94,000

	Motor Vehicles	Machines on hire-purchase	
Receiver's fees			7,000
Available for bank under fixed charges			87,000
Owing to bank			130,000
Shortfall at this stage			43,000
Estimated realisable values	10,000	20,000	
Less agents' costs	750	1,500	
	9,250	18,500	
Due to hire-purchase companies	12,000	16,000	
Shortfall to contra	2,750		
Surplus			2,500

Assets not specifically pledged

Stock		8,000	
Work in progress		28,000	
Fixtures and fittings		6,000	
Motor vehicles		7,000	
Plant & machinery		4,000	
		53,000	
Less estate agent's fees	6,000		
Receiver's fees	7,500	13,500	
			39,500
			42,000
PREFERENTIAL CREDITORS (including bank, £12,000)			32,000
Surplus available for bank			10,000
Balance due to bank (£130,000−£87,000−£12,000)			31,000
Shortfall to bank to be met by guarantor			(21,000)

Here, then, the combined estimated fees and costs total £28,750 and have the effect of:

1 Wiping out the surplus of £7,000 after paying the bank and leaving instead a shortfall to the bank of £21,000 to be met by its PMD guarantor.
2 Increasing the shortfall to the hire-purchase creditor from £2,000 to £2,750.
4 Wiping out the £7,000 surplus (as stated in 1, above) so that unsecured creditors will receive no dividend on their claims.

There will be no effect upon the preferential creditors in **3**, who will continue to have their claims paid in full.

The above illustration underlines the importance of allowing for realistic costs when reading an S/A with a view to assessing dividend prospects or liability under a guarantee.

It should be appreciated that the above example deals only with fees in a receivership. Where the debenture holder and preferential creditors are paid in full, leaving a surplus available for unsecured creditors, there will be the further fees of the liquidator to take into account in assessing final dividend prospects.

Vanishing Deposits

It is not necessarily the granting of credit which paves the way for a potential bad debt.

Just as there are two ways to tip an evenly balanced scale in one direction (take something off one side or add something to the other – the result is the same), a bad debt can be incurred by actually paying out money which then becomes irrecoverable.

A common example would be the giving of a deposit to secure a future order, where the order is never fulfilled and the contracting supplier becomes insolvent. The Poor Man's deposit has vanished, his order unfulfilled.

It is the general public who tend to be more at risk than the Poor Man trader. Everyone has heard of undercapitalised holiday firms collapsing, and cowboy fitted-kitchen or double-glazing companies going into liquidation, leaving hundreds of consumers with lost deposits.

The problem is: what can be done to prevent this kind of loss? What steps are available to the Poor Man depositor to help safeguard his deposit?

He should always attempt to retain some sort of charge over either his deposit or the goods themselves. Thus, where the goods already exist but, for whatever reason, he does not yet want to take delivery, he should require that the goods be isolated and clearly marked as his property. He should also obtain a letter confirming that position, at the same time as handing over the deposit.

Where the goods are not yet manufactured, he should require that a new bank account be opened into which his deposit is paid. The account should be a specially designated trust account in which the monies must remain until the order is fulfilled. The Poor Man can usually expect opposition to this request, particularly from suppliers who are so short of working capital that they need to utilise his deposit to enable them, in turn, to process his order.

The problem is that the Poor Man never knows whether *his* deposit is needed to complete some other customer's earlier-placed order. If it is, he will then be dependent upon the next Poor Man customer's deposit to process his own order.

This kind of financial juggling, known as 'teeming and lading' (not 'teeming and ladling' as it is so often miscalled) is one of the clearest indications of financial weakness, but because of its very nature can be easy to conceal.

It is to counteract this very problem that the request should be made to open the trust bank account – the point being that the trust monies so created will remain the property of the depositor until such time as the contract is fulfilled.

To be really safe, the depositor himself should be a co-signatory to the bank account, so that the monies cannot be moved out without his knowledge.

Although the Poor Man can expect problems when he starts talking about accounts 'impressed with a trust', the supplier's reaction could well be a pointer to just how secure or shaky is his own financial position.

In itself, there is nothing wrong whatsoever in any supplier requesting a deposit to secure a future order. It is probable that the supplier has never seen the prospective customer before and the deposit is both to encourage the customer to complete the contract and to minimise any chance of financial loss in the event of any breach.

On the other hand, security works both ways. What guarantee does the supplier have to offer that he will be able to fulfil his part of the bargain in due course?

The very request by the Poor Man depositor for special banking arrangements could be sufficient to reassure the supplier as to the Poor Man's integrity and to agree to waive the question of a deposit.

Another way to deal with a request for a deposit is to agree for the

93

monies to be held as stakeholder by either the Poor Man's or the supplier's solicitor until the goods are ready for delivery.

At the end of the day, whether or not to agree to hand over a deposit must be a matter of commercial judgment. The smaller and more newly established the supplier, the more cautious the Poor Man depositor should be.

If there be any doubt, he should be advised not to do it, and to go instead to a larger, more established concern, even if it is going to cost more money.

Where the deposit is to secure services – such as a future holiday – as opposed to goods, it will not be possible to take a charge over anything. Here, the Poor Man must rely upon the disciplines pertinent to the service in question, which are in force concerning depositors' money, and should satisfy himself that a special bank account is in operation to handle deposits in accordance with regulations laid down by a recognised regulating body. Thus, in the case of holiday deposits, the Poor Man should check the firm is a member of ABTA and that approved banking arrangements are in force.

Many firms offering a service either have to be, or can agree to be, regulated by an official body: by refusing to deal with anyone who is not so regulated, the Poor Man depositor at least has a chance of obtaining some sort of compensation should anything go wrong.

The Poor Man Investor

So much then for vanishing deposits – but what about monies placed by the Poor Man investor, usually because he is convinced he is 'on to a good thing' and will receive a much higher return upon his investment than anyone else in the country is prepared to offer?

> A secure income for life; 13 per cent return upon your money which will be used to purchase blue-chip investments.

How many individuals, particularly the elderly or retired, have been seduced by this kind of advertisement? Not just unlucky for some, unlucky for thousands. Who wants to fund the purchase of a yacht named the *Blue Chip*?

The problem with losses of this nature is that very substantial sums indeed can be involved – often the investor's life savings. If you are ever tempted by offers of above-average yield, stop and reflect upon the heartache and misery that has been suffered over the years by thousands of investors who have risked and lost their monies for the sake of a few extra per cent return.

In any event, what is the point of taking the risk? Suppose our Poor Man has £10,000 to invest and sees an offer of 13 per cent gross return upon his investment when the average return elsewhere is only $9\frac{1}{2}$ per cent. Should he be tempted? He should, first of all, work out the precise differential in simple figures.

Assume a composite tax rate of 30 per cent. The net return at the higher yield would equal £17.50 per week; at the lower yield £12.78 per week. Is it not worth his forgoing another £5 per week, rather than risk losing what could be his entire life savings of £10,000? Of course it is – so he should not do it: and if anyone advised him to invest, he should ask, 'What's in it for him?' Such a person will almost certainly be paid a commission as a percentage of that capital investment and our Poor Man might suggest that the adviser personally guarantee his money if he is so certain of its safety!

Never forget: the higher the yield from any new fund, then almost inevitably the higher the commission paid to the brokers to charm the Poor Man into placing his money into that particular fund. Now it would be hard enough for any new fund to earn sufficient profits over and above the established markets to enable it to pay any significantly higher rate of interest, but it becomes even more improbable when a large chunk of initial capital investment is paid out in excessive commissions.

Of course, there will always be the investment that pays above the market rate of interest and is both properly managed and perfectly safe. Even so, it is not for our Poor Man investor; it is *for the fortunate few who do not need the money in the first place and can afford to do without both the income and – should the worst come to the worst – their capital.*

Steps have been taken by the Government to try to protect the small investor. August 1988 saw the introduction of a fund of £100 million available in any one year to cover losses in the event of the failure of an authorised investment fund. However, claims are initially limited to a maximum of £50,000 per investor and, if £100 million should prove insufficient to cover all losses in any one year, this maximum of £50,000 could be proportionately reduced. (The Companies Act 1989 introduced additional measures further designed to regulate those operating under the Financial Services Act 1986.)

The Poor Man investor, who needs his capital to produce the income which supports his lifestyle, should stick to the recognised forms of investment. Schemes which yield high returns, however ingenious, are always open to Inland Revenue attack or change by subsequent legislation. After that, there is usually trouble.

When he looks at the temptingly worded glossy literature inviting him to part with his savings, he should recall and never forget the down-to-earth but so pertinent expression:

> Bullshit baffles brains.

It most certainly does and it is his brains 'they' are out to baffle!
His motto should henceforth read:

> I've cash to invest but it's money I need
> So I'm going for safety, forgoing all greed.

He might not get rich, but at least he will have peaceful nights!

5 Stories from the Author's Diary

Fred's Downfall

We will call our Poor Man haulage contractor Fred.

Fred's story demonstrates the impact that the VAT 15 per cent penalty (discussed on page 46) could have upon a Poor Man attempting to avoid bankruptcy and highlights the problems that arise from time to time when new legislation (such as that relating to VAT) is superimposed on existing law without sufficient thought being given to the possible side-effects.

Fred had been persuaded by a friend to buy some very expensive tipper wagons. His friend was a businessman who dealt in the purchase and sale of topsoil and, for whatever reason, decided he would prefer not to be involved in the bulk haulage that was entailed.

Fred agreed to acquire the requisite specialist vehicles and, between Fred, his friend and a sympathetic vehicle distributor, the paperwork was so arranged that no deposit was required. Fred signed the hire-purchase documents in his own name.

All went well for some months. Fred worked exclusively for his friend, who paid his invoices promptly, enabling Fred to discharge his monthly hire-purchase liability.

Then the inevitable happened. Fred, with all his eggs in one basket, had been sitting on a time-bomb. Unfortunately, it was a very large bomb, for his friend already had a string of insolvent companies behind him and now this latest topsoil supply company failed. Fred's friend was declared personally bankrupt.

Fred handed the vehicles back to the hire-purchase company, who promptly sold them and asked him for a cheque to make up the short-fall between the sale proceeds and the outstanding balance.

Fred had no chance – remember, he had not paid any deposit and tens of thousands of pounds were required. If only his (former) friend had not defaulted, owing him £36,000, everything would have been all right. He decided he would attempt a Deed of Arrangement with his creditors.

These were the days of the 15 per cent penalty and the total VAT involved as regards his ordinary trade creditors was around £6,000. Fred spoke with his relatives and was able to come up with the full amount. It seemed he could be saved.

Unhappily, the hire-purchase company then dropped its own bomb-shell. Although VAT is not added to hire-purchase instalments (as it is to lease payments) an arrangement had been reached with the Customs and Excise which allowed hire-purchase companies to apply an agreed formula to their outstanding instalments which entitled them to the VAT bad debt element thereby created. The Customs and Excise confirmed this hitherto unknown position.

The effect was disastrous. An additional £4,600 was required, which could not be raised. The hire-purchase company was both understanding and apologetic, but they had a house-rule: all losses had to be mitigated by the VAT bad debt relief and in all cases the debtor had to be formally bankrupted to obtain this relief in the absence of alternative funds being available.

Fred did the honourable thing; he spared them the trouble and expense and saved his relatives £6,000. He filed his own petition in bankruptcy.

Four months later, without prior notification, the VAT 15 per cent penalty was removed.

The Over-secured Joint and Several Guarantee

O show to me a guarantee of the joint and several kind
And I'll show you potential grief that's better left behind

PHF

Our second story concerns two men, partners in a professional office, whom we will call Partners A and B respectively.

The partners decided to purchase an investment property for £40,000. Partner A, who had some private capital, put up £20,000 whilst Partner B approached his bank for finance.

The bank agreed to make a loan of £20,000 available but only if they could take a fixed charge over the property itself and both partners entered into a joint and several guarantee. Neither partner

foresaw any problem; they were friends, business was good and the property, carefully chosen, was going to be very valuable in five or six years' time. They entered into the bank's form of standard guarantee and no one – including the manager – thought it necessary to take any further precautions.

A year or so later, Partner B entered into a speculative business venture which did not directly involve Partner A. He approached the bank, which agreed to support against his personal guarantee for £35,000. As part of the overall financial package, the bank also advanced £30,000 against his home, replacing an earlier building society borrowing. The house had a value of around £34,000.

Within two years, disaster struck. Partner B's new business venture had failed with a massive deficiency, his health collapsed so that he was, at least temporarily, unable to continue to earn a living and, by a cruel twist of fate, the effects of the miners' strike had extended to property values in his area. Within a short time he owed the bank £33,000 on his mortgage and could find no buyer for his house at an asking price of £30,000. He handed the bank the keys to the house and moved into rented accommodation.

The bank sent for Partner A and asked for his proposals with regard to B's indebtedness to the bank. Partner A did not understand – apart from the original £20,000 mortgage on the investment property, now happily reduced to £14,000, what had B's borrowings got to do with him?

The bank produced a copy of the original standard mortgage document, signed by A and which, to his horror, did not restrict the bank's charge to the original advance of £20,000. It extended to cover *all* B's (and of course his own) borrowings from the bank – both present and future! (This is absolutely standard procedure).

The property had by now a value of £65,000 and a sale would attract capital gains tax of £6,000. Partner A calculated the position as follows:

		£
Sale of investment property		65,000
Less cost of sale		4,000
		61,000
Due to bank on mortgage advance (originally £20,000)		14,000
		47,000
Value of B's house – say	27,000	
Outstanding mortgage	33,000	6,000
		41,000
Owing by B to bank under guarantee		35,000
		6,000
Capital gains tax due on sale of investment property		6,000
Net equity in property left for A		**Nil**

Poor Man Partner A ruefully calculated how much his kind action in sharing the investment property with his partner had cost in real terms: £20,000 originally invested, plus a share of after-tax profits which amounted to something over half as much again.

In the event, he managed to find some consolation (not a lot) in realising that had B's borrowings to the bank been any greater, he would – as explained in detail in the section on personal guarantees in chapter 4 – have had to find the £6,000 capital gains tax out of his own resources.

It might be thought that the above story could never happen in practice. Surely the position would be either fully understood or otherwise explained to the professional gentleman concerned, or the bank could never take advantage of an innocent, however crass, oversight by the guarantors? Nevertheless, the outline of the story is a faithful account of an actual occurrence. It is true that, under the special circumstances, the bank agreed to compromise with the partners, but the lesson remains.

It is to be hoped that it will never happen again. As a safeguard, whenever asked to sign a guarantee, the Poor Man guarantor should ensure that the guarantee is limited to a specific transaction and that the lender's interest in any security offered is limited to a maximum stated figure.

The Petition that Backfired

It is not always easy for a creditor to know what action to take to recover his debt in any specific instance.

There can be no doubt that DIY experts in law can find themselves with unexpected problems and it is always advisable – particularly (or as the lawyers might say, *a fortiori*) when substantial amounts of money are at risk – to seek legal advice at the earliest opportunity.

It is all very well for the Poor Man to know the importance of getting his blow in before anyone else, but does he attempt to obtain a judgment and then put the bailiffs in if his judgment is not paid, or does he issue a Section 123 notice and then petition the court for a compulsory winding-up order if the debt remains unpaid after twenty-one days?

In our third story, a creditor decided to follow the latter route and in due course issued his petition. The debtor responded with an offer to issue bills of exchange to the value of the debt to be payable at monthly intervals over the next few months, to the value of £20,000 per month.

The creditor accepted the compromise and agreed not to proceed with the petition. Now it is important to understand that once the petition has been made, it is up to the court whether or not it is allowed to be withdrawn. In this particular instance another, smaller creditor had already indicated he would support the petition and, following the withdrawal of the petitioning creditor, wished to adopt the petition. The court agreed to an adjournment of one month to enable the company to supply certain financial information but, finally, a winding-up order was made. By this time two of the bills of exchange had matured and the creditor thereby repaid £40,000 – half his debt.

In due course, the Offical Receiver handed over the case to an outside liquidator who, as luck would have it, was very experienced indeed; he lectured extensively upon the subject of insolvency and was the author of a number of technical discussion papers and a book on receivership. This expert liquidator wasted no time in writing to the creditor and spelling out the text of Section 522 of the Companies Act

1985 (since superseded by Section 127 of the Insolvency Act 1986), which reads:

> In a winding-up by the court, any disposition of the property of the company ... made after the commencement of the winding-up, shall, unless the court otherwise orders, be void.

We saw in chapter 2 that the winding-up of a company in compulsory liquidation is deemed to commence at the date of presentation of the petition and our Poor Man creditor had received £40,000 of the company's property – cash – after that date. Had the payments been made in the ordinary course of trade, the position could have been different, but in this case, all trade between the company and this creditor had ceased; it was, in effect, a means of collecting payment of an outstanding debt from an insolvent company.

The Poor Man creditor was obliged to repay the £40,000 to the liquidator.

If only he had managed to achieve payment without presenting that petition!

The Poor Man creditor should always seek to have the petition withdrawn as part of any agreement to accept payment in settlement of his debt. It is, however, up to the court to decide whether or not a petition may be withdrawn. Under such circumstances, the safest way forward is to insist that the directors settle the account personally – if necessary by taking the money from the company in their own name – so that any problems concerning breaches of Section 127 of the Insolvency Act 1986 will be theirs alone.

The above true story clearly demonstrates that what is good for the body of unsecured creditors generally can be anything but good for an individual creditor.

Compare it with the example given on pages 52–53, where placing the company into compulsory liquidation would have recovered

£250,000 for the creditors to the detriment of one creditor who, in that instance, had been 'preferred'.

Living with the new rules - AD

If it is difficult for the Poor Man client (PMC) to know which way to proceed, it is apparent that non-specialist practitioners can have an equally bad time when attempting to advise their PMC.

Now that insolvency appointments are restricted to the handful of practitioners holding licences, it is easy to understand why their partners and colleagues, with the usual exceptions, have abandoned any interest in learning the new rules. After all, what is the point of learning new legislation if you are not going to be allowed to put it into practice?

Understandable it may be, and it is true as Pope would have it, that

> ... A little learning is a dang'rous thing ...

None at all, however, can be fatal for the PMC. Inevitably, it will be to the partner in charge of his affairs that the PMC will first turn if he finds himself in any sort of financial difficulty. It is, therefore, very important that the non-specialist partner should have a thorough basic knowledge of the pitfalls that can face his PMC and the steps that should be taken to protect his interests.

Our two remaining stories demonstrate just how little is understood of the new legislation by the general practitioner. The first case history concerns a Poor Man company director, the second a Poor Man sole trader.

Directors' Unlimited Liability

'I've been sent to see you by the solicitors round the corner', said the man we will call Jamie. It seemed he was considering investing in a company which he believed was probably insolvent but where he was confident that the injection of his own expertise could 'turn it around'.

When asked what the statement of affairs showed, he answered that none had been prepared. (What – no Emergency Plan B?)

Ah well, apparently he had consulted the company's auditor, a partner in a most reputable firm of accountants, who had advised the present directors that it was safe to continue to trade 'provided there was light at the end of the tunnel'. (His very words.)

Those who have paid attention to the earlier sections of this book will be saying smugly, 'He's confusing the new concept of wrongful trading with the earlier concept of fraudulent trading'. Quite right, he was indeed, and thereby unnecessarily exposing his PMD client to a possible charge of wrongful trading which, as we now know, could place him on the road to personal bankruptcy.

Jamie was shown the paragraph in the book on wrongful trading – then in draft form – and went hotfoot back to the directors to warn them that the light at the end of their tunnel was in danger of being extinguished by the storm clouds gathering on the horizon.

Bankruptcy – the Avoidable Option?

In the first of these short histories, we saw how a quirk of fate frustrated our attempt to save a Poor Man from bankruptcy and how poor Fred would have been saved had he been a little luckier and managed to remain solvent for just another four months.

Today, AD, every Poor Man should have even more chance of avoiding formal bankruptcy, provided those to whom he turns for help are able to proffer the correct advice.

Early statistics would suggest that there is a long way to go. In 1987 there were 6,761 bankruptcy orders with just 403 IVAs and 29 DOAs. The comparative figures for 1988 were 3,937, 356 and 7, respectively.

Take the case of Charles. Charles was recommended to a local chartered accountant who had an enviable reputation, justifiably earned, as one of the most able practitioners in the area. A previous accountant had advised that there was no need to register a new business for VAT purposes. He was wrong and the Customs and Excise had asked Poor Charles for around £16,000 in back tax. This was bad enough, but to make things worse the Finance Act 1985 had introduced an automatic fixed penalty of 30 per cent of the tax due for failing to register!

(The 1988 Finance Act reduces the penalty to 20 per cent where registration is no more than 18 months late and down to 10 per cent where no more than 9 months late. Once again the Poor Man's fate is about to be decided by fluctuating outside factors.)

Poor Charles managed to persuade all his customers to accept retrospective VAT invoices, thereby simply moving around the principal VAT outstanding with no benefit whatsoever to the Customs and Excise. He was, however, stuck with the penalty and he did not have £4,800.

His new accountant tried everything in his power to persuade the Customs and Excise to drop their assessment, but to no avail.

Charles had no trade creditors, his only other outstanding liability being for a sum of under £2,000 which would shortly be due to the Inland Revenue. Unhappily, his only asset was £1,500 standing to his credit at the bank.

Now what the practitioner had failed to understand was that the Customs and Excise *had* to adopt the uncompromising posture of insisting upon assessing Poor Charles. They were dealing with public money; it was not their fault that previous accountants had given bad advice.

On the other hand, once an accounting position has been established, neither the Customs and Excise nor the Inland Revenue will oppose any sort of proper scheme of compromise, given genuine hardship and in the absence of any improper behaviour on the part of the debtor.

Here, then, was a case which cried out for an individual voluntary arrangement. There was even a sum of money readily available which would have been enough to cover the costs of the exercise. As it was, this otherwise brilliant accountant sent his new client down to the Official Receiver to file his own petition in bankruptcy.

Poor Charles became just another statistic.

6 Insolvency in Business - How to Avoid it

Starting a New Business

Our Poor Man Entrepreneur (PME) will need to carry out a great deal of preparatory work if he hopes to run a well-organised and profitable business.

Set out below are just some of the areas which will need due consideration and appropriate action. The PME should reproduce his own checklist, using the format below as a guide. Provision should be made alongside each individual heading for the PME to make a note of the appropriate action which has been taken against each section.

Initial assessment

1 Consider whether your own ability and experience, personal circumstances and health are compatible with the proposed venture.

2 With regard to the products and services which you intend offering, consider:

   a What makes you think you are likely to succeed where others may well have tried and failed.

   b Assuming that you are able to create the necessary demand for your products or services, are you able to be competitive while remaining profitable? Are you risking transgressing the law in any area in an effort to achieve your objectives?

   c Consider the potential risks involved in joining the ranks of the 'self employed', particularly if you have family responsibilities. Weigh the potential dangers of insolvency against your hopes of profitable trading. In particular, if you are contemplating trading with the benefit of limited liability, be certain that you have a thorough understanding of the very onerous responsibilities of a company director and learn about the consequences to a director who is convicted of wrongful trading.

Make sure you have read and understood the first five chapters of this book!

Obtaining finance

1 Prepare a business plan for presentation to bank managers and other potential financial backers.

2 The business plan should be presented so as to demonstrate to any potential lender that:

a You have a thorough knowledge of the business and understand the required financial disciplines.

b Your product or service is technically sound and that there is a likely demand at a realistic price.

c You are budgeting from the start to ensure adequate finance and that adequate security is available to cover the required borrowings.

d Realistic budgets project profitability, which will be adequate to demonstrate long-term growth while at all times providing you with a living and servicing both the interest and repayment requirements of the projected borrowings.

3 The business plan should therefore include:

a A curriculum vitae for the PME and any proposed partners or senior members of staff in the business.

b Full product or service details, including specification, price and sales forecasts. Give as much information as possible in support of the sales forecast, e.g. copies of relevant marketing surveys or letters of commitment from prospective customers.

c A cash flow forecast, preferably on a four-weekly or monthly basis, for at least the first year of trading. The forecast should clearly identify all sources of capital introduced by the PME and should allow for interest on borrowings and provide a degree of flexibility to allow for contingencies.

d A profit forecast covering the same period.

e Details of the bases upon which the cash flow and profit forecasts have been prepared, e.g. 'The cash flow anticipates payment to suppliers in the month following supply but payment being received from customers two months following supply. The profit forecast anticipates an increase in wages of 5 per cent after the first six months and a general provision of 3 per cent has been incorporated to cover potential bad debts.'

109

     f A detailed schedule of capital expenditure required to set up the business with details of any additional expenditure which will be necessary as the business increases in size.

     g A forecast balance sheet showing the anticipated position of the business at the conclusion of the period covered by the cash flow and profit forecasts.

4 It is probable that the PME will require expert advice from an accountant to prepare and reconcile cash flow and profit forecasts. More of this later.

5 The PME should always remember when preparing his figures that no lender is impressed by reckless optimism. It is far better to be cautiously prudent in the preparation of a business plan, showing borrowings sufficient to requirements, than to be over-optimistic, particularly in the forecasts of sales and cash flow.

Open a business bank account

1 It may be necessary for you to shop around for the best deal as, from time to time, banks often introduce special start-up terms for new small businesses.

2 Discuss with your accountant and bank manager the overall financing of the business. Consider a long-term bank loan as opposed to borrowing everything on current account. Compare leasing with hire purchase and enquire about the availability of development capital.

3 Try to find out as much as possible about any grants which may be available locally or generally. Incentives come and go but it is nearly always possible to find some sort of available grant or incentive scheme. For example the PME would be extremely upset to discover, after the event, that an area just a mile away from his chosen site was designated an enterprise zone and that he had lost out on substantial grants.

4 The PME's accountant or bank manager should be able to assist. Information should also be sought from the local Job Centre, Small Business Centre or any local Department of Trade and Industry (DTI) office.

5 Once this area has been fully explored, it should then be possible to incorporate any available grants or incentives within the above-mentioned cash flows and profit forecasts.

Legal and constitutional matters

1 The PME will need to decide on the form which his business is going to take. Sometimes circumstances limit the selection but the traditional alternatives are as follows:

a Sole trader. Here the PME becomes the sole proprietor and therefore, while enjoying all of any profits, becomes personally responsible for all the liabilities of the business.

b Partnership. This will mean that the PME trades with one or more other persons. A partnership agreement can either be verbal or subject to a written agreement. When the latter is contemplated legal advice should be sought. It is important that the PME should realise that every partner is legally liable for all the debts of the partnership, so that if any one partner fails to pay his share, the creditors may look to the other partners to meet the liability.

It is an old saying that 'partnership is the worst ship ever to set sail'. This does not mean that the PME should never contemplate partnership, but it should warn him to be extremely cautious.

c Limited liability. Should the PME decide to trade with the benefit of limited liability then, in law, the company will become his employer as a legal entity in its own right with the PME becoming its employee as a director.

One of the prime reasons for trading with limited liability is to ensure that the liabilities of the company are the responsibility of the company, with the shareholders liable to lose only the share capital they subscribed.

Elsewhere in this book, various pitfalls have been considered which could give rise to claims against directors personally, despite the intended shield of limited liability. In addition, Section 24 of the Companies Act 1985 can impose personal liability on a member (shareholder) if the company trades for over six months with only one member. (There must be at least two members.)

2 Legal advice should always be sought by the PME if his proposed venture involves:

a Partnership or shareholders' agreement.

b Takeover of an existing business.

c Purchase or lease of business premises.

d Local planning or environmental regulations.

Taxation
The PME will need to:

1 Inform the local Inland Revenue office as soon as he starts in business.
2 Decide upon his accounting year-end. (Professional advice can be most important, particularly for sole traders or partnerships.)
3 Consider whether it will be necessary to set up a scheme for PAYE. Special care needs to be taken if payments for casual labour are contemplated or if any part of the business is classed as building or contracting. In the latter case a special certificate may be required from the Inland Revenue.
4 Consider the impact of National Insurance Contributions. The regulations covering NIC vary infrequently but they are always complicated and, here again, professional advice is essential.

Value added tax
The PME will need to consult with his local Customs and Excise office or accountant to consider:

a Whether registration is required or, alternatively,
b Registration is preferable in the particular circumstances.
c Penalties for late registration.
d How to account for VAT on sales (output tax) and to reclaim VAT charged on purchases and expenses (input tax).
e Completion of the necessary VAT returns.

The importance of dealing correctly with VAT cannot be over-emphasised. The penalties and retribution which may be exacted by HM Customs and Excise for transgressions of the law need to be clearly understood by every PME from the outset.

Insurance
Many a PME has, to his regret, largely ignored insurance as being an unnecessary waste of money. Others have found that they are not properly insured only when it is too late.

An experienced insurance broker should be able to advise on all aspects of insurance requirements. Moreover, his service should be free as he will receive a commission from the insurance companies with whom the business is introduced upon his advice.

The law requires that minimum insurance be taken out covering the use of motor vehicles and for claims by employees against physical injury or illness which may result in the course of their employment. Insurance must also be taken out covering members of the public against accidents which might occur on the business premises (public liability insurance).

The current insurance certificate should be prominently displayed at the business premises.

In addition to the above, the prudent PME will also consider insurance covering:

a Damage to premises and contents, including stock, following fire, flood, theft or accident.
b Consequential loss (loss of profits) as a result of a disruption in business arising out of a claim in a) above.
c Loss of money.
d Damage to third party property.
e Loss of earnings following a protracted period of inability to work.
f 'Key-Man' insurance covering senior personnel.

One final area of insurance which is never too soon to consider is that of a personal retirement pension. The PME's insurance broker, in conjunction with his accountant, will be able to advise upon current tax effective schemes for setting money aside out of profits.

Books and records

Should the PME decide to trade with the benefit of limited liability, then the law requires that the company maintain proper books and records which adequately disclose the state of the company's affairs on a daily basis.

Notwithstanding the requirements of the law, it is essential that every PME maintain books and records which are adequate to ensure that up-to-date accurate financial information can be abstracted to enable the performance of the business to be closely monitored. This is particularly important in the early years of a new business and simplicity should always be the main criterion.

Modern microcomputers can and do work wonders in many instances, but their misuse or lack of suitability for a specific function can cause headaches and problems for both management and financial advisers and can confuse and be a hindrance rather than a help in extracting accurate financial information. The PME should

113

always remember that a computer is little more than a sophisticated calculating and recording machine and that the information it gives out is no better than the combination of the quality of the initial input and the software programme. If the information which it churns out is nonsensical then the fact that it provides that information quickly and efficiently is of little help!

If in the first instance the PME is unable to understand simple basic handwritten accounting records, then the information on a microcomputer is unlikely to provide the answer to his problem; he needs accounting advice.

The need for professional advice

The PME reading this chapter will have noticed from time to time the reference to taking advice from an accountant, solicitor or bank manager. The importance of early advice cannot be over-emphasised; the time to consult with the professional advisers is when considering the business venture – not after the commencement of trade. Any costs involved should prove a wise investment. Seek the advice of an accountant who will undertake to provide you with a free 'no obligation' interview and perhaps also greatly reduce fees during the early years of trading.

In addition to the established professionals, there are a number of government-backed advice centres which have been set up with a specific aim of assisting small businesses.

How to Avoid Financial Failure

In the first section of this chapter, we have considered some of the steps that should be taken by any PME before commencing to trade, and in chapter 1, pages 3–5, we looked at some simple but essential preventative measures which should help the PME from incurring bad debts, which could, in turn, bring down his own business. In the following chapters, we looked at various steps which can be taken should insolvency appear on the horizon once trading has been under way for some time.

The question every PME wants answering, however, is 'how do I avoid financial failure'? Sadly, there is no magic wand and no simple solution.

Many years ago, a young accountant was discussing one of his firm's client's year-end results. The client, a small jobbing builder, suddenly said to the young accountant for no apparent reason, 'You know, your boss is a marvellous accountant; he gave me some wonderful advice twenty years ago.'

Seeing that the client had no intention of enlarging any further upon his statement, the young accountant asked of him, 'What sort of advice did he give you?'

'Well,' said the builder, 'I had been going to buy a dumper and he said to me, "Don't do it Wallie – you could go bust." Marvellous man, wonderful advice.'

'Then what did you do instead?' enquired the young accountant.

'Oh, I bought the dumper anyway,' said the builder.

'I'm afraid I don't follow,' said the accountant. 'In that case how come the boss and his advice are so marvellous?'

'Ah well, you see,' said the builder, 'My friend, he bought a dumper as well – and he went bust!'

There is no real answer to such logic, although within that simple statement lies a very great understanding: given a similar set of circumstances, it is down to the ability of management to ensure survival.

If insolvency practitioners have any special awareness over and above that enjoyed by their non-specialist peers, it is a realisation that the line between profitability and insolvency is often so fine as to be quite frightening. Every successful PME needs to develop this sense of awareness, which should enable him to adapt to changing circumstances and, hopefully, anticipate trouble before it actually arrives.

Charles Dickens' Mr Micawber demonstrated at least a partial awareness when he spoke his immortal lines recognising that sixpence either way made all the difference between happiness and misery.

Such commercial awareness is an understanding that few business failures are brought about through an isolated occurrence, such as sustaining a large bad debt or someone else's discovery that quartz can regulate a watch mechanism more cheaply and accurately than conventional, mechanical methods.

Times change; sometimes the pace of change quickens and the PME who fails to adapt to changing conditions is likely to be among the first to suffer the financial consequences. Every PME should learn from history. The economy rarely remains stable; every few years the country experiences an economic boom followed by a few years of recession. The secret is to make the most of the boom years but to anticipate the recession before it arrives and be in a position to weather the storm.

It might help the PME to a better understanding if he likens the economy to a carousel spinning round and round. The driving force behind the carousel is confidence in the economy. As confidence builds, so we see foreign investments being made in our economy and as this confidence rises so more and more people in effect jump on the carousel, which turns at ever increasing speed.

Now, there is only so much money in any economy and thus only a certain amount of money to go round, but the greater the confidence, the faster spins the carousel with that money changing hands more often. As confidence wanes, people stop buying and stop investing, in effect jumping off the carousel, so that we have a slowing down and the start of a recession.

So what are the signs of recession that any observant PME should look out for? There are a number of tried and tested signs, and when they start to appear together, every PME should be preparing for a change of direction.

A change in the state of the housing market is one of the first signs of a booming economy. As the carousel spins faster, there is a greater demand for houses and a sharp increase in house prices, usually way above the level of any increase in inflation. Then High Street shops report record levels of sales as consumer spending reaches new limits, financed by ever-increasing personal credit card borrowings.

And then we see the warning signs. As people continue to scramble onto the carousel spending as much money as they can, while house prices reach almost absurd and impossible levels in some parts of the country, interest rates start to rise by one or two points.

'No need to be concerned,' the PME reads in his paper or hears on the news, 'just a touch of the brake to slow down the rapid increase in personal debt which is accumulating and help prevent any increase in inflation.'

Remember our 'Acid Test' on page 11? 'If things are so good, why are things so bad?'

The PME can expect before long to see mortgage rates rise and the property market stagnate. As higher interest rates begin to bite, the man in the street jumps off the carousel and spends less money in the shops. The shops, selling less, buy less, so that demand for manufactured goods falls almost overnight. Our carousel of economy is becoming, for many, a vicious circle of financial problems.

So what can the PME do to minimise the risk of financial failure? He should:

1 First of all ensure that he starts his business on a sound commercial footing, by at least covering all the various aspects detailed in the first part of this chapter.

2 Once his business is underway, he should ensure that the simple disciplines detailed on pages 2 and 4 concerning the

    avoidance of bad debt and, if appropriate, reservation of title, are installed and maintained.

3 Having established a profitable business, he should try to develop a commercial awareness and take care

    a not to expose his business to violent changes in the economy;

and

    b to anticipate such changes and be prepared to adapt accordingly.

By way of example, let us take the case of the PME whose business is trading profitably and enjoying buoyant sales. The PME decides to approach the owner of his business premises, as he likes the idea of owning the property. Property prices are high and rents are rising so that the idea appeals to both parties and a sale is agreed.

The mortgate repayments appear modest enough, about 25 per cent higher than the original rental, and all goes well for about six months, when suddenly the economic bubble bursts, sales dry up, property becomes unsaleable at anything but a give-away price and interest rates rise by 60 per cent, forcing up the monthly payments to a point which strains cash flow to the limit. So what value has ownership of the property now? Rents have stabilised (as they do in times of recession) and life as a humble tenant would have been far preferable to this new ownership.

Not that the ownership of property is to be discouraged: far from it. Timing is, however, important (remember King Canute on page 22?) and where a company has to borrow heavily to achieve a purchase, it becomes vital.

In this example a number of factors have combined to cause financial difficulties; viz:

- the decision to acquire the property, coupled with
- the downturn in the economy, which itself brought about
- an increase in interest rates, thereby affecting mortgage repayments; and
- a drop in sales causing reduced profitability.

In this instance what our PME should have done was to have timed his property acquisition to coincide with the *start* of the increase in momentum of the economy's carousel. To attempt to jump on when it is spinning at maximum revolution is always to court disaster.

We have already followed the results of higher interest rates through to the lowering of demand for manufactured goods. In theory, this would have no effect upon our own manufacturing industry, provided the drop in demand was equalled by an equivalent drop in imports.

In practice, such a dream is an impossible reality; better that our own industry looks outwards to new markets abroad, exporting to counteract shrinking home sales.

The key words have to be:

- anticipation
- timing
- adaptation and, where necessary,
- change

There is an often quoted but important story of the two businessmen on holiday abroad. One day, in the middle of nowhere they spotted a tiger racing towards them. One man immediately opened his pack and taking out his running shoes quickly put them on.

'Why are you bothering to do that?' enquired his colleague. 'You've no chance of outrunning the tiger.'

'I have no intention of trying to outrun the tiger,' said his companion. 'I only have to outrun you.'

This truism applies in business. The PME who keeps his business lean, fit and ready to move at speed where necessary, will survive where his competitors fail.

If despite all other precautions and efforts insolvency raises its head, the PME should consult with a specialist sooner rather than later. Although prevention is always better than cure, for the PME simply to sit back and do nothing could, at best, rob him of any chance of saving the business and, at worst, place him in further peril through (however innocently) transgressing insolvency law.

Every PME should always remember that nothing ever stays constant. It can often be more difficult to maintain profitability within a business than it was to start and build up the business in the first place.

The secret in contemplating change or adaptation is for the PME to think through a manoeuvre as he would a move in a game of chess. What are the likely consequences of his action? What might be the unlikely consequences? Anticipating and avoiding the potential disadvantages of planned future strategy will give the PME at least a sporting chance of avoiding financial failure.

Epilogue

All the examples in the book are drawn from real life. In one or two instances the names have been changed or the facts adapted to protect the innocent. In the majority of cases a similar approach has been adopted so as not to embarrass the guilty.

The book started with an acknowledgment that insolvency was not a humorous topic. Even so, the seriousness of any single financial position ought really to be viewed in the context of a larger, continuing world.

The plight and feelings of a certain Poor Man were once discussed by the Leeds practitioner who made the famous preferential address recounted in chapter 4. Summing up on the subject, he turned to a fellow professional and said,

> ... at the end of the day, when the Great Auditor in the sky draws up the final balance sheet, do you know what the answer will be?
> A lemon, dear boy; a lemon.

Perhaps he was right.

INDEX

'Acid test', the 11, 71
Administration order
  as alternative to receivership 43
  as a way forward 14, 15
  general 43
  not long term 48
  procedure 47
  reasons for requesting 48
  and rights of action 43
Administrative receiver, *see*
  Receivership
Annual return
  delay in filing 3
  failure to file 7
Arm's length, need to maintain in
  transactions 7
Assets, risk to personal 24
Authorised insolvency
  practitioner 12, 14, 17, 53

Bad debts 2
Bank
  choice of independent
    accountant by 25, 26
  choice of receiver by 21, 28, 35
  decision to appoint receiver 24
  formal demand to repay 28
  formal request to appoint
    receiver 21
  importance of charges 18, 19
  need to have debenture to
    appoint receiver 24
  request for additional

    security 25
  request for independent
    appraisal 25
  reluctance to appoint
    receiver 19
  security requirements 16
Bankruptcy
  acts of 60
  background 55
  the road to 55
'BC and AD', the options 56, 57
Book debts, collection
  procedures 5
Books of account, need to
  maintain 7
'Branch roads', *see* 'Scheme under
  Section 425'; Voluntary
  arrangement, company

Capital gains tax in a
  liquidation/receivership 20
Case histories
  'Fred's downfall' 98
Case histories *continued*
  'The over-secured joint and
    several guarantee' 99
  'The petition that
    backfired' 102
  'Bankruptcy – the avoidable
    option?' 105
  'Directors' unlimited
    liability' 105
Charges – fixed and floating, *see*

Fixed/ Floating charges
'Clayton's case' 39, 84
Committee, liquidation 77
Companies House search 3, 4, 41
Compulsory liquidation 14, 49, 50
   as opposed to voluntary 49, 51
   as weapon available to unsecured creditors 36, 50
   commencement 53, 103
   petition to wind up, *see* Winding-up petition
Costs of liquidation 88
Costs of preparing statement of affairs 22
Creditors
   order of priority 79
   position of, in a receivership 32
   preferential, *see* Preferential creditors
   secured, *see* Secured creditors
   unsecured, *see* Unsecured creditors
   voting rights of secured 74
Creditors' meetings
   attendance at 72
   convened for differing purposes 72
   voting at by proxy 72
Crossroads, the, 'Emergency plan B' 6, 10

Debenture
   definition 19
   not necessarily bank that takes 37, 39
   over director's loan 38
   validity of 39
Debenture holder 19, 57
Deed of arrangement 56, 58
Deposits, 'vanishing' 92
   protecting 92–4
Directorship
   pitfalls, the 6
   serious offences 8

shadow 7
Disqualification to act as director 7–9
Dividend prospects in liquidation, assessment, *see* Unsecured creditors: dividends to

'Emergency Plan B' 6, 10

Fees payable to
   liquidator/receiver 17, 75, 77, 88, 92
   trustee in bankruptcy 89
Fixed charges 15, 16
   assets covered by 17
Floating charges 18
   assets covered by 18
   past consideration 39
   validity 39, 40, 41, 47
Fraudulent trading 7, 8

Guarantee
   joint and several 10, 70, 71, 99
   personal 7, 10, 67
   precautions before signing 70
   taxation pitfalls 68
   to support company borrowing 16
Guarantor
   of debenture 84
   of hire-purchase agreements 88

Hire-purchase agreement, consolidation 32, 87, 88

Insolvency (corporate)
   definition of 11
   preventative measures 2
   road to 2
   way forward 14
Investor, 'Poor Man' 94

Liability, contingent 11
Licensed insolvency practitioner,
    see Authorised insolvency
    practitioner
'Light at the end of the tunnel' 8,
    105
Limited liability, origins 2
Liquidation
    committee 77
    compulsory, *see* Compulsory
        liquidation
    conversion to company voluntary
        arrangement 45
    creditors' voluntary 14, 49, 50
    date of commencement of 53
    members' meeting to place
        company into 35
    members' voluntary 14, 49
    reasons for postponing following
        receivership 34, 35
Liquidation following receiver-
    ship 35
Liquidator
    acts for all creditors 35
    appointment of (by voting) 49,
        77
    requirement to withdraw if
        receiver appointed 36
    right to handle charged
        assets 36

Meeting of creditors
    agenda 77
    following receivership 20, 33
    held to appoint liquidator 34,
        50, 77
    reason for convening 72
    speaking at 76, 77
Moratorium, creditors' 43, 44

Newhart v. *Co-operative Commer-
    cial Bank Limited* 36

Official Receiver, as provisional
    liquidator 51

Personal guarantees, *see*
    Guarantees
Petition to wind up, *see* Winding-
    up petition
Pitfalls for a company director 6
Preferences
    challenge by liquidator or
        administrator 41
    definition 6, 63
    intention to prefer 6
    period 39, 51, 53
    relevant time 6, 41, 59
    time scales 6, 39, 63
    voidable
        against liquidator or
            administrator 39, 41
        against trustee in
            bankruptcy 59, 62
Preferential creditors
    bank for wages paid 83
    definition of 32
    list of 19
    receiver's duty to pay 23, 32,
        35
    relevant date following
        administration 49
    risk to directors if not paid 23
    shortfall to 84
Proof of debt 74
Proxy
    form of 72, 74, 75
    voting by 72

Receiver
    acts as agent of the com-
        pany 21
    arrival of 28
    buying business from 31
    need to co-operate with
        director 29, 30, 34, 37
    right of fixed-charge holder to
        appoint 17
    right of floating-charge holder to
        appoint 19
Receiver (administrative) under

floating charge 18
Receiver under fixed charge 17
Receivership (administrative)
  appointment of receiver 24
  appraisal before
    appointment 25
  as a way forward 14, 15
  costs of 90
  creditors' committee 34
  debenture required to effect
    appointment 19, 24
  decision to trade 19, 30, 33
  directors' remedies upon
    disagreement 37
  effect upon directors'
    position 19
  general 15–43
  major benefits of 20
  meeting of unsecured
    creditors 20, 33
  'questions and answers' 24–43
  receiver's power to manage 19,
    30
  receiver's right to control
    assets 36, 37
  request for 19, 21
  sale of business 30
  security by way of a charge 16
  statement of affairs in, need
    for 21, 27, 34
  'The first few days' 30
  warning signs of impending 25,
    84
Redundancy payments and employees' claims 85, 86
Reference, trade 3
Register of charges 4
Repayments of advances secured
  by fixed and floating charges,
  demand for 18, 28
Report to Department of Trade
  upon conduct of directors 51
Reservation of title 4, 5, 31, 82

Scheme under Section 425 of the
  Companies Act 1985 14, 42,
  44

'Search' at Companies House 3,
  4, 41
Security, collateral 16, 24
Shadow director 7
Share capital, in statement of
  affairs 87
Starting a new business,
  groundwork 107 ff.
Statement of affairs
  appraisal of 82
  classes of creditor 79
  comparison with balance
    sheet 78
  cost of preparation of 22
  creditors, significance of order of
    priority 83
  flow chart 80
  general 11, 26, 34, 78
  need for 22
  redundancy payments and
    employees' claims 85
  significance to guarantor 22, 23
  worked example 81
Statutory declaration of
  solvency 14
Steps necessary following
  insolvency 10

Trade protection associations 3,
  66, 75
Trade references 3
Transfer at undervalue 6, 40, 47,
  59, 62, 63
Trust, constructive 74
'Twice blest he whose cause is
  just ...' 5, 44, 102

Undervalue, transfers at 6, 40,
  47, 59, 62, 63
Unsecured creditors
  dividends to 32, 42, 52, 78, 88,
    92
  moratorium granted by 44
  risk, exposure to 32

'Vanishing deposits' 92
VAT
  'bad debt relief' 20, 32, 46, 88
  certificate by receiver 20, 32
  hire-purchase payments, on 99
  not available under CVA or
    Section 425 scheme 46
  penalty for failure to
    register 106
  penalty, 'the 15 per cent' 46,
    59, 61, 98
Voluntary arrangement com-
    pany 14, 42, 45
  individual 57, 61, 107

Voluntary liquidation
  creditors' 14, 49
  members' 14, 49
Voting at creditors' meetings 50,
    72

'Wages Account' 25, 84
Wages claim, preferential 83
Warning signs of possible receiver-
    ship 25, 84
Winding-up petition 36, 41, 50,
    102
Wrongful trading 7, 8, 9, 56, 105